Series/Number 07-089

MULTIPLE COMPARISON PROCEDURES

LARRY E. TOOTHAKER
University of Oklahoma

SAGE Publications
International Educational and Professional Publisher
Newbury Park London New Delhi

The author is grateful to the Literary Executor of the late Sir Ronald A. Fisher, F.R.S. to Dr. Frank Yates, F.R.S. and the Longman Group Ltd. London for permission to reprint Table B from their book Statistical Tables for Biological, *Agricultural and Medical Research* (6th edition 1974).

For information address:

SAGE Publications, Inc.
2455 Teller Road
Newbury Park, California 91320
E-mail: order@sagepub.com

SAGE Publications Ltd.
6 Bonhill Street
London EC2A 4PU
United Kingdom

SAGE Publications India Pvt. Ltd.
M-32 Market
Greater Kailash I
New Delhi 110 048 India

Printed in the United States of America

Toothaker, Larry E.
Multiple comparison procedures / Larry E. Toothaker.
p. cm.—(Quantitative applications in the social sciences; 89)
Includes bibliographical references.
ISBN 0-8039-4177-3 (pb)
1. Multiple comparison (Statistics) I. Title. II. Series: Sage university papers series. Quantitative applications in the social sciences; 89.
QA278.4.T66 1993 92-29596
519.5′35—dc20 CIP

96 97 98 99 00 01 10 9 8 7 6 5 4 3

When citing a university paper, please use the proper form. Remember to cite the current Sage University Paper series title and include the paper number. One of the following formats can be adapted (depending on the style manual used):

(1) TOOTHAKER, L. E. (1993) Multiple Comparison Procedures. Sage University Paper series on Quantitative Applications in the Social Sciences, 07-089. Newbury Park, CA: Sage.

OR

(2) Toothaker, L. E. (1993) *Multiple comparison procedures* (Sage University Paper series on Quantitative Applications in the Social Sciences, series no. 07-089). Newbury Park, CA: Sage.

CONTENTS

Series Editor's Introduction vii

1. Introduction 1

Example: Helping Behavior 2

Multiple Comparisons 2

Definition 2

Dimensions of Classification 5

Types of Error Rate, Hypotheses, and Mean Configurations 8

Types of Error Rate 8

Types of Hypotheses 10

Types of Population Mean Configurations 12

Types of Statistics 12

t Statistic 12

Range Statistic 13

F Statistic 14

Mean Difference 16

Confidence Intervals 16

Use of *t* 17

Orthogonality of Multiple Comparisons 17

SAS and SPSS 21

SAS 21

SPSS 25

2. Multiple Comparison Procedures 27

An MCP That Controls α Using ERPC: *Usual t* 27

Simultaneous Test Procedures 31

Dunn 31

Tukey 32

Scheffé 34

Stepwise Methods 35

Newman-Keuls 35

Ryan (REGWQ) 38

Protected Tests 41
Protected *t* Test (Fisher's LSD) 41
Shaffer-Ryan 42
Fisher-Hayter 43
All Treatments Compared With a Control 44
Dunnett 44
Summary 45

3. Comparison of MCPs **46**
Critical Values and Power 46
Miller Data 49
Usual t 49
Dunn and Tukey 50
Scheffé 51
Newman-Keuls 51
Ryan 53
Shaffer-Ryan 55
Fisher-Hayter 55
Dunnett 55
Summary 55

4. Violations of Assumptions and Robustness **57**
Unequal Sample Sizes and Variances 59
Unequal Sample Sizes 59
Tukey-Kramer 60
Unequal Population Variances 61
Research on Other MCPs 61
Special MCPs 62
The GH Procedure 62
Example 63
Robustness to Nonnormality of Classical MCPs 64
Summary 66

5. Multiple Comparisons for the Two-Way ANOVA: Factorial or Randomized Blocks **66**
Example: Study Technique and Cognitive Style 67
Control of α 68
Main Effect Means 69
MCPs on Main Effect Means 69
SAS and SPSS 71
Interaction Tests Versus Cell Means Tests 72

Interaction Tests 72
Cell Means Tests 74
Critical Values for Cell Means Tests 75
Summary 78

Appendix: Tables of Critical Values 79

Notes 88

References 92

About the Author 96

SERIES EDITOR'S INTRODUCTION

Suppose the researcher wants to assess effects across three or more treatment groups. For example, Professor Green, in charge of Psych 101, randomly assigns students equally to three different instructional conditions (independent study, discussion, lecture), then measures test performance. A one-way ANOVA, by yielding a significant F test, causes rejection of the null hypothesis of equality of the group means. This result suggests there is an overall effect from instructional condition. But Green cares more about the differences between the groups; for example, Is the independent study group mean significantly different from the discussion group mean? Is the discussion group mean different from the lecture group mean? In other words, the professor seeks different, or multiple, comparisons.

The desire for multiple comparisons makes the statistical analysis rather complex. However, Dr. Toothaker's lucid explication of multiple comparison procedures (MCPs) reduces that complexity to a series of manageable choices. In Chapter 2, he intelligently reviews 10 MCPs available for one-way ANOVA, summarizing their key features, strengths, and weaknesses. For instance, he notes that while the *usual t* procedure has the highest power, it is most prone to Type I error. Besides explaining all the procedures, he shows how to obtain them with the statistical packages of SAS and SPSS. This step-by-step lesson is invaluable, given that SAS, for example, offers 15 MCPs. Besides discussing the computer routines themselves, Dr. Toothaker also notes some pitfalls of the packages, such as the fact that the critical values SAS gives each MCP are not comparable. Helpful cautions such as this pepper the monograph.

How to choose among the competing MCPs? In Chapter 3, to guide that choice, Dr. Toothaker systematically compares the different procedures in terms of their critical values and, by extension, their power. Certain are faulted, such as the popular Newman-Keuls method. Others, however, such as the Ryan procedure, fare quite well. The final chapters extend MCPs into two neglected areas: robustness when ANOVA assumptions are violated, and the problems of application in the two-way ANOVA.

This monograph nicely complements others in the series, particularly *Analysis of Variance* (Iversen & Norpoth, 1987), *Multivariate Analysis of Variance* (Bray & Maxwell, 1985), *Multiple Comparisons* (Klockars & Sax, 1986), *Experimental Design and Analysis* (Brown & Melamed, 1990), and *ANOVA: Repeated Measures* (Girden, 1992). In itself, it should be required reading for any researcher engaged in multiple comparison procedures. The quality of direction Dr. Toothaker provides the reader is exceptional.

—*Michael S. Lewis-Beck*
Series Editor

MULTIPLE COMPARISON PROCEDURES

LARRY E. TOOTHAKER
University of Oklahoma

1. INTRODUCTION

If you do research with more than two groups, you will want to compare these groups. Consider these examples: market research concerned with which of three types of television commercials is most effective, psychotherapy research concerned with comparing four different treatments for depression, and educational research concerned with which of three methods used in teaching reading yields the best performance.

If the research question is about equality of the means of these groups, then you usually will need multiple comparisons. The one-way ANOVA, as an overall test of equality of the means of the groups, will simply answer the question, Is there any difference in the groups?[1] This overall test does not address the issue of which groups are significantly different when compared two at a time.

In the market research example above, for instance, perhaps the subjects were randomly assigned to one of three types of television commercials. After viewing the commercials, the subjects were asked to indicate their intention to buy the advertised product by allocating 100 points among the advertised brand and three competitors. The dependent variable was the number of points the subject gave to the advertised brand. The one-way ANOVA on the dependent variable would test for equality of the three means of the types of television commercials. If the overall F test was significant, the overall null hypothesis of equality of means would be rejected, and you could conclude that some differences existed in the three means. However, you likely want to determine which of the three types of commercials differ significantly from the others. This could be answered by testing which of the three means differ significantly when compared two at a time.

Example: Helping Behavior

A study in developmental psychology was concerned with the focusing of responsibility on children and its effect on their attempts to help another child in apparent distress.[2] The manipulated variable was the instructions the children were given, and the dependent variable was a rating of helping behavior. A total of 42 first-grade students were randomly assigned to one of three groups, $n = 14$ per group. Subjects in the first group were informed that there was another child alone in the next room who had been warned not to climb on a chair. This group was called *indirect responsibility* (IR). In addition to the story told to the subjects in IR, subjects in the second group were informed that when the adult left, they were in charge and to take care of anything that happened. This group was called *direct responsibility one* (DR1). Subjects started a simple task, and the adult left the room. Next, there was a loud crash from the next room and a short time of crying and sobbing. In the third group, direct responsibility two (DR2), subjects had the same instructions as DR1, but there were also calls for help. From behind a one-way mirror, two raters gave ratings on helping behavior. The scale was from 1 (no help) to 5 (went to next room), and the dependent variable was the average rating from the two raters.

Table 1.1 gives the data, the means (and standard deviations) rounded to two decimal places, and the ANOVA summary table. Figure 1.1 shows the plot of the group means for the three groups in the helping behavior example.

Using $\alpha = .05$, there are significant differences in the three group means. However, the ANOVA is not designed to show you the location of those significant differences. This example will be used to illustrate each multiple comparison procedure in Chapter 2.

Multiple Comparisons

DEFINITION

A comparison on J means is a linear combination of the means,[3] such as the difference between two of the J means, or the difference between one mean and the average of two other means. The name *multiple comparisons* shows that there can be many different comparisons. To express the definition symbolically, a comparison is

TABLE 1.1
Helping Behavior Example (n = 14 per group)

	IR	*DR1*	*DR2*
	3	3	4
	2	5	3
	1	4	5
	4	3	5
	3	5	3
	2	3	3
	3	4	4
	4	3	4
	4	3	4
	2	5	4
	2	5	5
	3	4	2
	1	1	3
	2	3	1
Means (standard deviations)	2.57 (1.02)	3.64 (1.15)	3.57 (1.16)

ANOVA Table

Source	*df*	*SS*	*MS*	*F*	*p*
Between groups	2	10.05	5.02	4.08	.0247
Within groups	39	48.07	1.23		

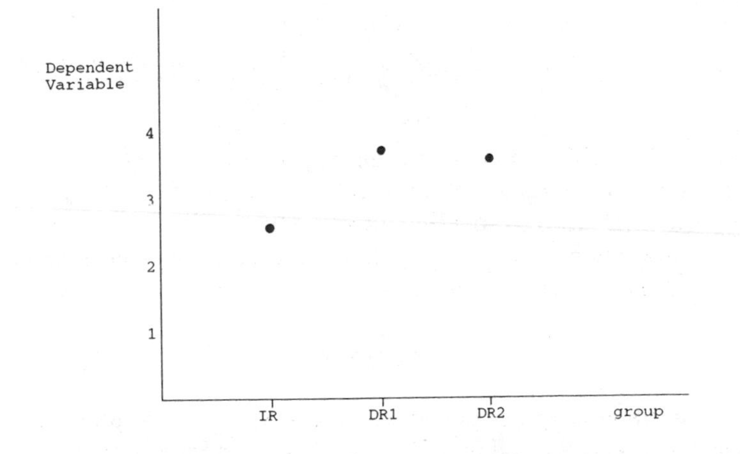

Figure 1.1. Group Means, Helping Behavior (Staub, 1970)

$$\Psi = c_1\mu_1 + c_2\mu_2 + \ldots + c_J\mu_J = \sum_{j=1}^{J} c_j\mu_j \tag{1}$$

where the sum of the weights, the c_j's, equals zero, but not all of the c_j's are zero. Note that the definition of a comparison is given in terms of population means. The sample statistic that is an estimator of the population comparison is given as

$$\hat{\Psi} = c_1\overline{Y}_1 + c_2\overline{Y}_2 + \ldots + c_J\overline{Y}_J = \sum_{j=1}^{J} c_j\overline{Y}_j \tag{2}$$

where the c's are the same as for the population comparison. Note that the sample and population comparisons are identical except that sample means are substituted for population means, and that there are n observations in each of J groups.

For $J = 3$ means, suppose you want to examine the following differences: mean one compared to mean two, mean one compared to mean three, and mean one compared to the average of means two and three. The comparisons could be given as

$$\begin{aligned}
\hat{\Psi}_1 &= \overline{Y}_1 - \overline{Y}_2 = (1)\overline{Y}_1 + (-1)\overline{Y}_2 + (0)\overline{Y}_3 \\
\hat{\Psi}_2 &= \overline{Y}_1 - \overline{Y}_3 = (1)\overline{Y}_1 + (0)\overline{Y}_2 + (-1)\overline{Y}_3 \\
\hat{\Psi}_3 &= \overline{Y}_1 - \frac{\overline{Y}_2 + \overline{Y}_3}{2} = (1)\overline{Y}_1 + (-\tfrac{1}{2})\overline{Y}_2 + (-\tfrac{1}{2})\overline{Y}_3 .
\end{aligned} \tag{3}$$

Examine the weights in the first comparison: $c_1 = 1$, $c_2 = -1$, and $c_3 = 0$. Here, as in any comparison, the sum of the c's is zero, $1 + (-1) + 0 = 0$.

Consider the mean, variance, and shape of the sampling distribution of a sample comparison. The population mean, or long-run average, of any sample comparison is given by

$$\mathrm{E}(\hat{\Psi}) = \Psi \tag{4}$$

and, with equal sample sizes and the usual ANOVA assumption of equal group variances, the variance of a sample comparison is given by

$$\sigma^2_{\hat{\Psi}} = \sigma^2_e \sum_{j=1}^{J} \frac{c_j^2}{n}. \tag{5}$$

We estimate the variance of a sample comparison by using MS_W as an estimate of σ_e^2 giving

$$\text{estimated } \sigma^2_{\hat{\Psi}} = \hat{\sigma}^2_{\hat{\Psi}} = MS_W \sum_{j=1}^{J} \frac{c_j^2}{n}, \tag{6}$$

where

$$MS_W = SS_W/df_W, \tag{7}$$

within degrees of freedom is $df_W = J(n - 1) = N - J$, and

$$SS_W = \sum_{j=1}^{J}\sum_{i=1}^{n} Y_{ij}^2 - \frac{\sum_{j=1}^{J}\left(\sum_{i=1}^{n} Y_{ij}\right)^2}{n}. \tag{8}$$

Finally, the sampling distribution of a sample comparison is normally distributed; that is, it has the shape of a normal distribution. You will need the mean, variance, and shape information about the sampling distribution of a sample comparison later, when we begin to form test statistics using sample comparisons. First, let's examine some different ways to classify multiple comparisons.

DIMENSIONS OF CLASSIFICATION

There are many ways to describe multiple comparisons, and these lead to many dimensions on which they can be classified. Note that the following classifications describe one of the following: the comparisons themselves, the types of statistics that you could compute on the comparisons, the types of error rate control, or the different reference distributions to which you could compare these statistics.

Number of comparisons. The first classification dimension is the number of comparisons computed.[4] You could do a large number of the possible comparisons or some small subset of all possible comparisons.

Orthogonal versus nonorthogonal.[5] *Orthogonal* generally indicates lack of relationship between two variables, but a specific mathematical definition indicates two vectors that are at right angles to each other. The orthogonality being considered here is between the comparisons themselves: For the comparisons in Equation 3, is the first comparison orthogonal to the second comparison? You can have a group of comparisons that are all orthogonal to each other or that possess some nonorthogonality. This issue will be discussed more fully below.

Pairwise versus nonpairwise. Pairwise comparisons are those in which you examine the means in pairs, where the weights are 1 and −1 for two of the J means and zero for all others. A pairwise comparison is simply a difference between two means. Comparisons one and two in Equation 3 are examples of pairwise comparisons. The maximum number of pairwise comparisons that you could compute on J means is given as $J(J-1)/2$. So for $J = 5$ means, there are $5(5-1)/2 = 10$ pairwise comparisons. The type of comparison labeled *nonpairwise* is any comparison that is not a pairwise comparison. Comparison three in Equation 3 is an example of a nonpairwise comparison. The term *general* will stand for any comparison, pairwise or nonpairwise.

Planned versus post hoc. Planned (or a priori) comparisons are those that you planned to do before the results were obtained. Often, planned comparisons are based on predictions from the theory that has led to the research project. Post hoc (or a posteriori or postmortem) comparisons are those you compute after you inspect the results. With post hoc comparisons you can choose comparisons based on the results, such as doing only the largest three comparisons. Post hoc comparisons may or may not have a theory base for inclusion in the study. Chapter 2 will discuss when this topic is important in the use of a multiple comparison procedure.

Stepwise versus simultaneous test procedures. Some multiple comparison methods depend in part upon another statistic. For example, a procedure may allow you to compute comparisons only if the overall F is significant, or may allow you to compute one comparison only if some other comparison is significant. Comparison methods with such dependencies are called stepwise methods, because computation of the comparisons proceeds in steps. Multiple comparison methods that do not have such dependencies are called nonstepwise or simultaneous test procedures (STPs), because all of the comparisons may be computed simultaneously.

Types of statistics. Many of the multiple comparison procedures differ with respect to the statistic and/or the theoretical reference distribution used to make the inference. Indeed, some of the methods differ with respect to the type of inference that you can make, such as tests of hypotheses or interval estimation. These issues will be dealt with in a later section.

Types of error rate. There are two basic types of error rates: α-control for each comparison and α-control for some group of comparisons. The latter category contains several different subtypes of error rate. Additionally, there are different types of null hypotheses and configurations of population means that could occur. The different types of error rate, hypotheses, and mean configurations will be discussed in a later section.

Some of the literature on multiple comparison procedures (MCPs) contains popular misconceptions that some combinations of these categories cannot occur. Most of these classification categories can occur together, depending upon the choices you make. You could choose multiple comparisons that are planned and control error rate for the group of comparisons. You may choose comparisons that are orthogonal and not planned or do post hoc comparisons controlling error rate for each comparison. Although some combinations are impossible, such as all pairwise comparisons and orthogonal comparisons (see below), and some combinations may be unusual, most are not impossible or forbidden. Note, however, that sometimes planned comparisons are connected with control of α for each comparison.

Some of these classification categories are not open to your choice simply because the research question dictates the nature of the comparisons themselves. Possible examples are the number of comparisons computed, whether or not the comparisons are orthogonal, and whether or not the comparisons are pairwise. Other issues, such as type of null hypothesis and configuration of population means, are dictated by the populations of data. Often, whether the comparisons are planned or post hoc is dictated by the research question, but sometimes you have this choice. You can choose type of error rate, type of statistic, and stepwise or STP, with the type of error rate being the most basic and perhaps most important decision. As in basic hypothesis testing, the important concepts in the area of MCPs are power and control of α.

Types of Error Rate, Hypotheses, and Mean Configurations

TYPES OF ERROR RATE

The complexity of the topic of multiple comparisons is largely due to the fact that you want to do *multiple* comparisons. If you want to do only one comparison, many of the complexities disappear. Control of error rate is one such issue. The control of error rate can be accomplished in several different ways for multiple comparisons, and you must choose one of them for each research project. Basically, the choice of error rate control is choosing what value of α' to assign to each comparison. Such choice also influences the power of the eventual statistic.

Error rate per comparison. One of the two basic categories of α-control is to set error rate for each comparison, which is called error rate per comparison (ERPC).[6] You accomplish this by setting $\alpha' = \alpha$ at the chosen level, typically .05, for each comparison. Then you would choose α-level critical values for the appropriate statistic for each comparison.

One problem with controlling α using ERPC is that the probability of at least one Type I error increases as the number of comparisons (C) increases. That is, if $\alpha' = .05$, then for one comparison, the probability of at least one Type I error is .05, but for two comparisons, it is closer to .10; for three comparisons, .15; and so on. For C orthogonal comparisons each at level α', this is shown as

$$\text{p(at least one Type I error)} = 1 - (1 - \alpha')^C \leq C\alpha' , \qquad (9)$$

where $C\alpha'$ is the approximate upper bound on p(at least one Type I error). If the C comparisons are not orthogonal, then $1 - (1 - \alpha')^C$ is an upper bound to p(at least one Type I error). Empirical research shows that p(at least one Type I error) is fairly close to $1 - (1 - \alpha')^C$ for all possible pairwise comparisons, which are not all orthogonal.

While the bad news for ERPC is that the probability of at least one Type I error is large, the good news is that the power is also large.[7] Control of error rate using ERPC gives higher power than any other method of error rate control, but at the expense of high p(at least one Type I error).[8] What is true in basic hypothesis testing is true for use of MCPs. There is a trade-off between control of α and β: Allowing high probability of at least one Type I error (high α) gives high power (low β).

Error rate per family. The second of the two basic categories of α-control is to set α for some group of comparisons. Error rate per family (ERPF) is the first of two types of α-control that do so for a group—or, equivalently, family—of comparisons.[9] ERPF is the average number of erroneous statements (false rejections, Type I errors) made in a group (family) of comparisons, thus it is the only definition of error rate that is not a probability. ERPF is achieved by selecting values of α' such that they add up to α. For example, if α' is constant for all comparisons, then for C orthogonal comparisons each at level α', ERPF is equal to $C\alpha'$. This method of controlling error rate appears in the logic of the Dunn method, to be discussed in Chapter 2.

Error rate familywise. The second type of α-control that functions for some group of comparisons is error rate familywise (ERFW). ERFW is a probability and is defined as the probability of at least one Type I error, p(at least one Type I error), given earlier in Equation 9. When choosing small values for p(at least one Type I error), such as .05 or smaller, if a method accomplishes control of α using ERFW or ERPF, it usually approximately accomplishes the other. If the average number of erroneous statements (ERPF) is kept small, then the probability of an erroneous statement (ERFW) is also kept small. Thus the basic decision you face with respect to α-control is whether to control error rate for each comparison (ERPC) or some group of comparisons (ERPF or ERFW).

First, examine the relationships among these three different types of α-control. If α' is used for each of C comparisons, then using ERPC gives $\alpha = \alpha'$, using ERFW gives $\alpha \le 1 - (1 - \alpha')^C$, and using ERPF gives $\alpha \le C\alpha'$. Putting these together gives

$$\alpha' \le 1 - (1 - \alpha')^C \le C\alpha' , \tag{10}$$

which easily leads to

$$\text{ERPC} \le \text{ERFW} \le \text{ERPF}. \tag{11}$$

For example, if we set $\alpha' = .01$ for $C = 5$ orthogonal comparisons, then ERPC = .01, ERFW = .049, and ERPF = .05 (Table 1.2).

Second, from Table 1.2, for small α' and reasonable C, ERFW and ERPF are fairly close. Note that control of ERPF at $\alpha = .05$ always gives ERFW of slightly less than .05. In practice, if one of these "family"

TABLE 1.2
Various Values of Type I Error Rate

Number of Orthogonal Comparisons (C)	α'	*ERPC*	*ERFW*	*ERPF*
5	.01	.01	.049	.05
5	.010206	.010206	.05	.05103
10	.005	.005	.04889	.05
10	.0051162	.0051162	.05	.051162
10	.05	.05	.40	.50

rates is controlled at $\alpha = .05$, the other will be very close to .05. Also, if you set $\alpha' = .05$ for $C = 10$ orthogonal comparisons, then ERPC = .05, ERFW = .40, and ERPF = .50, illustrating that control of α for each comparison (ERPC) leads to excessive α for a group of comparisons (ERFW or ERPF). Finally, note that ERPF serves as an upper bound for ERFW.

TYPES OF HYPOTHESES

The concept of "types of hypotheses" concerns the equalities that exist in the population means. That is, attention is paid to which means are equal rather than to which means are different.

Overall null hypothesis is the first type of hypothesis. An overall null hypothesis exists if all of the J means are equal. This is the null hypothesis tested by the overall F test, thus the name *overall null hypothesis.* Another term for the overall null hypothesis is the *full null hypothesis.*

Multiple null hypotheses exist if the overall null hypothesis is not true, but more than one subset of equal means do exist. The means must be equal within the subset, but there must be differences between the subsets. Then each of these subsets represents a null hypothesis. If there are M multiple subsets of means with equality within the subset, there are M multiple null hypotheses. For example, if $J = 4$, and means one and two are equal but different from means three and four, which are equal (see Figure 1.2), then there are $M = 2$ null hypotheses.

Partial null hypothesis is the configuration that exists when the overall null hypothesis is not true, but some population means are equal. For example, examine Figure 1.3. For $J = 4$, if the first three means were equal but the fourth were larger than the first three, there would be a

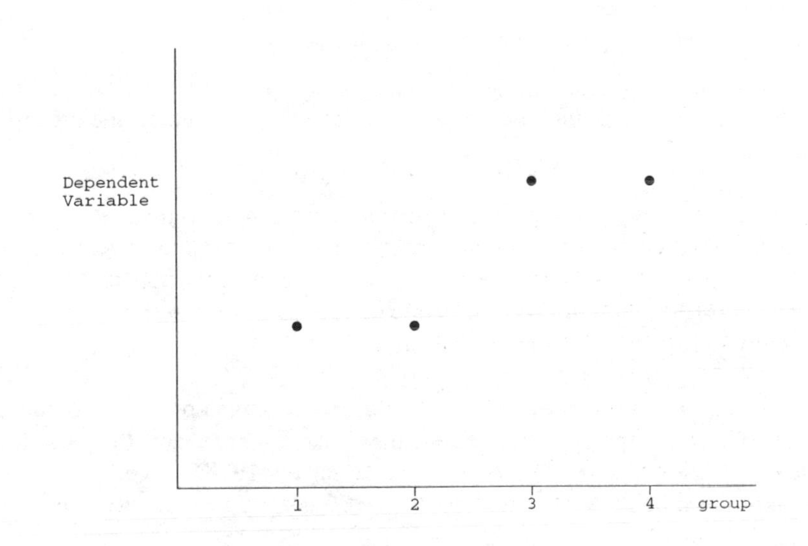

Figure 1.2. Group Means, Multiple Null Hypotheses

partial null hypothesis in the three equal means. Note that partial null hypothesis, the larger set, includes multiple null hypotheses: Every multiple null hypothesis is a partial null hypothesis, but not the reverse.

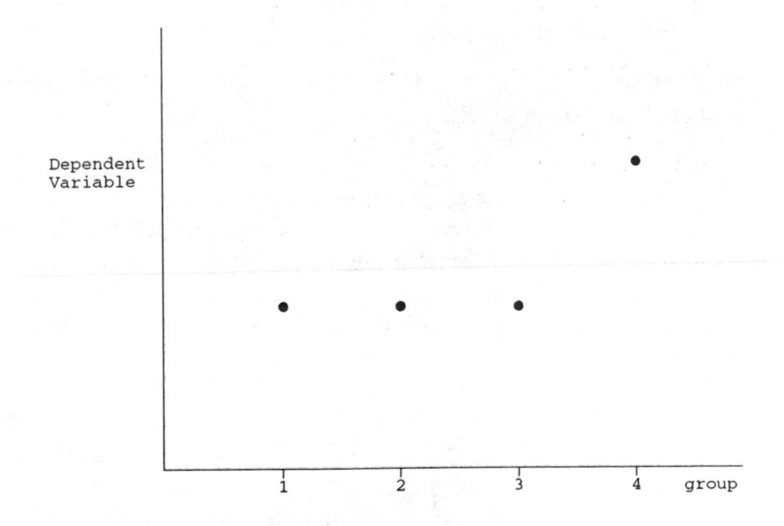

Figure 1.3. Group Means, Partial Null Hypothesis

TYPES OF POPULATION MEAN CONFIGURATIONS

When we were examining types of hypotheses, attention was paid to which means were equal. Now we want to attend to which means are unequal.

Minimum range configuration. A minimum range configuration has the first half of the means equal and the second half equal but different from the first half (Ramsey, 1978). For odd J, the first half is defined as means one through $(J + 1)/2$. An example of minimum range means would be if $\mu_1 = \mu_2 = 20$ and $\mu_3 = \mu_4 = 40$.

Maximum range configuration. A maximum range configuration has the first mean the lowest, the last mean the highest, and the middle means the average of the first and last (Ramsey, 1978). An example of maximum range means would be if $\mu_1 = 20$, $\mu_2 = \mu_3 = 30$, and $\mu_4 = 40$.

Equally spaced configuration. In this configuration of population means, each succeeding ordered mean is a fixed increment higher than the preceding mean, in a stair-step fashion. An example would be if $\mu_1 = 20$, $\mu_2 = 25$, $\mu_3 = 30$, and $\mu_4 = 35$, with a constant difference of 5 from the preceding mean.

Types of Statistics

Part of the complexity of the topic of MCPs is that there are several different statistics, most of which are interchangeable.[10]

t STATISTIC

For any given comparison, you know three crucial pieces of information about its sampling distribution: the mean, the variance and how to estimate the variance, and that the shape of the sampling distribution is normal (see Equations 4-6). Given this information, you can form a t statistic for any given comparison,

$$t_{\hat{\Psi}} = \frac{\hat{\Psi} - \Psi}{\sqrt{\text{MS}_\text{W} \sum_{j=1}^{J} \frac{c_j^2}{n}}}. \tag{12}$$

The hypothesis to be tested by t usually is

$$H_0: \Psi = 0, \tag{13}$$

where

$$\hat{\Psi} = \bar{Y}_j - \bar{Y}_{j'}. \tag{14}$$

Thus for equal sample sizes and pairwise comparisons, the t statistic simplifies to

$$t_{\hat{\Psi}} = \frac{\bar{Y}_j - \bar{Y}_{j'}}{\sqrt{\frac{\mathrm{MS_W}}{n}(2)}} \quad \text{for any } j \neq j'. \tag{15}$$

If there is only a single comparison of interest to you, then given the usual ANOVA assumptions of normality, equal variances, and independence, the t statistic can be used to test this hypothesis using a critical value from the t distribution with df = $\mathrm{df_W}$ (see Appendix Table B). When you have more than one comparison, the t statistics must be referred to appropriate critical values for the MCP selected from those methods given in Chapter 2. Again, the selection of the MCP will depend upon your choice of error rate. The t statistic can be used for any of the methods discussed in this text.

RANGE STATISTIC

One of the basic statistics used in MCPs is called the range statistic or the Studentized range,[11] and has the following formula

$$q = \frac{\bar{Y}_j - \bar{Y}_{j'}}{\sqrt{\frac{\mathrm{MS_W}}{n}}} \quad \text{for any } j \neq j'. \tag{16}$$

The Studentized range has two parameters, J = number of means and $\mathrm{df_W}$. Appendix Table C gives critical values of the Studentized range for various values of J and $\mathrm{df_W}$ for $\alpha = .05$ and $\alpha = .01$.

For pairwise comparisons, there is a very simple relationship between the t and range statistics:

$$t = \frac{\overline{Y}_j - \overline{Y}_{j'}}{\sqrt{\frac{MS_W}{n}\sum_{j=1}^{J} c_j^2}} = \frac{q}{\sqrt{2}} = \frac{\overline{Y}_j - \overline{Y}_{j'}}{\sqrt{\frac{MS_W}{n}}}\,\frac{1}{\sqrt{2}}\,. \tag{17}$$

The difference in the two formulas is that t has as its denominator the estimated standard deviation of the comparison, which includes the $\Sigma c_j^2 = 2$, for pairwise comparisons, while q has as its denominator the estimated standard error of one of the means in the comparison. For pairwise comparisons, the Σc_j^2 always equals 2 because the c_js are 1 and −1 for the two means being compared and zero for the other means. Thus the denominator of the t is the estimated standard error of the difference between two sample means. A simple form of Equation 17 shows $t = q/\sqrt{2}$, which allows you to use the t statistic as a substitute for q with any MCP using a range statistic. Once the t statistic is computed, compare it to a q critical value divided by the square root of 2; that is, compare t to

$$\frac{q_{J,\, df_W}}{\sqrt{2}}\,. \tag{18}$$

For example, the q critical value for $J = 4$ and $df_W = 20$ is 3.96, so dividing by the square root of 2 gives 2.80. You would compare the t statistic to 2.80, giving results equivalent to comparing the q statistic to 3.96.

F STATISTIC

Some MCPs use another statistic, the F statistic,[12] for a comparison. This F is related to the t statistic by the formula $t^2 = F$, thus it has only one degree of freedom in the numerator. Because every F statistic is the ratio of two mean squares, an F statistic for a comparison will be a ratio of a mean square for the comparison divided by MS_W. The sum of squares and mean square for a comparison can be found by starting with the relationship $t^2 = F$, and rearranging some of the terms as given in

$$t^2 = \frac{(\hat{\Psi} - \Psi)^2}{\frac{MS_W}{n}\sum_{j=1}^{J} c_j^2} = \frac{(\hat{\Psi} - \Psi)^2 \Big/ \left(\sum_{j=1}^{J} c_j^2/n\right)}{MS_W} = F\,. \tag{19}$$

From Equation 19, because F is a ratio of two mean squares, we have

$$\text{SS}_{\hat{\Psi}} = \text{MS}_{\hat{\Psi}} = (\hat{\Psi} - \Psi)^2 \Bigg/ \left(\sum_{j=1}^{J} c_j^2/n \right), \tag{20}$$

where the MS and the SS are equal because there is only one degree of freedom for the comparison.

An example will help to show the relationships among the three statistics given up to this point. Suppose that there are $J = 4$ groups with $n = 6$ observations in each group. If $\text{MS}_\text{W} = 12.98$ and the four sample means are computed as

$$\overline{Y}_1 = 54.1, \quad \overline{Y}_2 = 39.8, \quad \overline{Y}_3 = 37.5, \quad \overline{Y}_4 = 29.3 \tag{21}$$

and you want to compare means one and two, then the weights are 1, −1, 0, 0. With a null hypothesis of the population comparison equal to zero, then you can compute t as

$$\hat{\Psi} = \overline{Y}_j - \overline{Y}_{j'} = 54.1 - 39.8 = 14.3$$

$$t = \frac{\overline{Y}_j - \overline{Y}_{j'}}{\sqrt{\frac{\text{MS}_\text{W}}{n}(2)}} = \frac{14.3}{\sqrt{\frac{12.98}{6}(2)}} = \frac{14.3}{\sqrt{4.3267}} = \frac{14.3}{2.08} \tag{22}$$

$$t = 6.87\,.$$

Computation of q is similar, and is related to t

$$q = \frac{\overline{Y}_j - \overline{Y}_{j'}}{\sqrt{\frac{\text{MS}_\text{W}}{n}}} = \frac{54.1 - 39.8}{\sqrt{\frac{12.98}{6}}} = \frac{14.3}{\sqrt{2.1633}} = \frac{14.3}{1.47}$$

$$q = 9.72 \tag{23}$$

$$t = \frac{q}{\sqrt{2}} = \frac{9.72}{1.4142}$$

$$t = 6.87\,.$$

You can obtain $t = 6.87$ directly or by first computing q and then dividing by the square root of 2. You can compute F by

$$F = \frac{\text{MS}_{\hat{\Psi}}}{\text{MS}_\text{W}} = \frac{(\hat{\Psi} - \Psi)^2 \Big/ \left(\sum_{j=1}^{J} c_j^2/n \right)}{\text{MS}_\text{W}} = \frac{(14.3)^2/(2/6)}{12.98}$$

$$= \frac{204.49/0.3333}{12.98} = \frac{613.47}{12.98} \tag{24}$$

$$F = 47.26$$

$$t = \sqrt{F} = \sqrt{47.26} = 6.87\,.$$

Because t is related to F, the square root of F gives $t = 6.87$, the same value obtained by directly computing t.

MEAN DIFFERENCE

Another statistic on a multiple comparison is often called a *mean difference.* The comparison, which is a mean difference for a pairwise comparison, is used directly, rather than changing it into a t, q, or F statistic. The mean difference form is shown here as it relates to both t and q:

$$\hat{\Psi} = \bar{Y}_j - \bar{Y}_{j'} = t_\text{crit}\sqrt{\frac{\text{MS}_\text{W}}{n}(2)}$$

$$\hat{\Psi} = \bar{Y}_j - \bar{Y}_{j'} = q_\text{crit}\sqrt{\frac{\text{MS}_\text{W}}{n}}\,, \tag{25}$$

where t_crit and q_crit are appropriate critical values that depend upon the MCP selected.

CONFIDENCE INTERVALS

The statistics already given here have been presented primarily as test statistics appropriate for testing the hypothesis $H_0\!:\psi = 0$ for each comparison. All of the MCPs given in this text are able to provide you with a test of this hypothesis. However, if you want to compute an interval estimate of the population comparison, then some MCPs are not appropriate. That is, some of the MCPs are used only to test hypotheses and cannot give interval estimates of the population comparisons. For those methods that can give confidence intervals, the interval is given as

$$\hat{\Psi} - \text{crit}\left(\sqrt{\frac{\text{MS}_\text{W}}{n}\sum_{j=1}^{J} c_j^2}\right) \le \Psi \le \hat{\Psi} + \text{crit}\left(\sqrt{\frac{\text{MS}_\text{W}}{n}\sum_{j=1}^{J} c_j^2}\right), \tag{26}$$

where crit is an appropriate critical value, such as t, $q/\sqrt{2}$, or $\sqrt{F}$. The upper and lower values of the interval also can be expressed as

$$\hat{\Psi} \pm \text{crit}\left(\sqrt{\frac{\text{MS}_\text{W}}{n}\sum_{j=1}^{J} c_j^2}\right). \tag{27}$$

If you desire to both test hypotheses and obtain interval estimates, you can use the confidence interval to test the hypothesis that the comparison is zero by rejecting H_0 if the interval does not contain zero.[13] For example, if an interval has been computed as (−.50, 2.95), then you would not reject H_0; if the interval were (.73, 3.47), then you would reject H_0.

USE OF *t*

Because all of the statistics presented in this section can be transformed to the t statistic, the MCPs presented in Chapter 2 will use t and transform the appropriate critical values. If you use $t = q/\sqrt{2}$ and $t = \sqrt{F}$, then you can compute a common statistic, t, and compare critical values to determine the most powerful MCP, as will be shown in Chapter 3.

Orthogonality of Multiple Comparisons

From the definition given earlier, you might remember that *orthogonal* is loosely defined as "unrelated" and more mathematically as when two vectors are at right angles. Because of its use in the area of multiple comparisons, we have to define and discuss orthogonality of comparisons. However, the bottom line is that this topic is not as important as its amount of coverage would indicate. For all of its practical utility to multiple comparisons, we could stop here. However, as stated earlier, we must consider the topic, but let's keep in focus its relative lack of importance as an issue in MCPs. First let's find out if orthogonality has anything to do with choice of comparisons.

You might ask, Which comparisons should I compute? One answer would be to compute the comparisons that are dictated by your research questions. If your question is, Which of these J means are different? then you will likely compute all possible pairwise comparisons, and they are not all orthogonal to each other. If your question is, Do these two treatment groups differ, on the average, from the control group, and are the two treatments different? then you will make two comparisons. One comparison will examine the difference between the control mean and the average of the two treatment means and the other will examine the pairwise difference of the two treatment means; these two comparisons are orthogonal. Thus choice of which comparisons to compute is dictated by the research questions, not by whether or not the comparisons are orthogonal.[14]

Orthogonality of multiple comparisons is considered for pairs of comparisons, two at a time. If you have three comparisons in a group of comparisons, orthogonality is determined for comparisons one and two, comparisons one and three, and comparisons two and three. If the sample sizes are equal, orthogonality of any two comparisons is determined by the weights on the means. If

$$\sum_{j=1}^{J} c_{1j}c_{2j} = 0\,, \tag{28}$$

then comparisons one and two are orthogonal.[15] Here c_{1j} and c_{2j} are the weights for comparison one and two on the jth mean. If the sum of the product of the weights is not zero, then the comparisons are nonorthogonal. Consider the following comparisons two at a time and determine which pairs are orthogonal if the n's are equal:

$$\begin{aligned}
\hat{\Psi}_1 &= \bar{Y}_1 - \bar{Y}_2 \\
\hat{\Psi}_2 &= \bar{Y}_1 - \bar{Y}_3 \\
\hat{\Psi}_3 &= \bar{Y}_3 - \bar{Y}_4 \\
\hat{\Psi}_4 &= \bar{Y}_1 - \tfrac{1}{2}\bar{Y}_3 - \tfrac{1}{2}\bar{Y}_4\,.
\end{aligned} \tag{29}$$

First, you should write the c's for all J means for all of the comparisons in a table, and then compute the sum of products for each pair of comparisons:

	*j*th mean			
	1	2	3	4
comparison 1	1	−1	0	0
comparison 2	1	0	−1	0
comparison 3	0	0	1	−1
comparison 4	1	0	−½	−½

$$1\ vs.\ 2{:}\ \sum_{j=1}^{J} c_{1j}c_{2j} = (1)(1) + (-1)(0) + (0)(-1) + (0)(0) = 1$$

$$1\ vs.\ 3{:}\ \sum_{j=1}^{J} c_{1j}c_{3j} = (1)(0) + (-1)(0) + (0)(1) + (0)(-1) = 0$$

$$1\ vs.\ 4{:}\ \sum_{j=1}^{J} c_{1j}c_{4j} = (1)(1) + (-1)(0) + (0)(-\tfrac{1}{2}) + (0)(-\tfrac{1}{2}) = 1 \quad (30)$$

$$2\ vs.\ 3{:}\ \sum_{j=1}^{J} c_{2j}c_{3j} = (1)(0) + (0)(0) + (-1)(1) + (0)(-1) = -1$$

$$2\ vs.\ 4{:}\ \sum_{j=1}^{J} c_{2j}c_{4j} = (1)(1) + (0)(0) + (-1)(-\tfrac{1}{2}) + (0)(-\tfrac{1}{2}) = 1.5$$

$$3\ vs.\ 4{:}\ \sum_{j=1}^{J} c_{3j}c_{4j} = (0)(1) + (0)(0) + (1)(-\tfrac{1}{2}) + (-1)(-\tfrac{1}{2}) = 0\,.$$

So comparison three is orthogonal to comparisons one and four, but none of the other pairs of comparisons is orthogonal. Within the set of all possible pairwise comparisons, most of the comparisons are not orthogonal to each other, such as comparisons one and two above.

For a set of J means, the maximum number of comparisons that are all orthogonal to each other is $J - 1$. You may find several sets of comparisons in which all $J - 1$ comparisons are orthogonal to each other, but once you find such a set, there can be no more than $J - 1$ orthogonal comparisons within that set. Note that there are at most $J - 1 = 3$ comparisons in each set of the following two examples of sets of orthogonal comparisons for $J = 4$.

<u>*set one*</u>

$$\Psi_1 = (1)\mu_1 + (-1/3)\mu_2 + (-1/3)\mu_3 + (-1/3)\mu_4$$

$$\Psi_2 = (0)\mu_1 + (1)\mu_2 + (-1/2)\mu_3 + (-1/2)\mu_4$$

$$\Psi_3 = (0)\mu_1 + (0)\mu_2 + (1)\mu_3 + (-1)\mu_4$$

<u>*set two*</u>

$$\Psi_4 = (1)\mu_1 + (-1)\mu_2 + (0)\mu_3 + (0)\mu_4 \qquad (31)$$

$$\Psi_5 = (0)\mu_1 + (0)\mu_2 + (1)\mu_3 + (-1)\mu_4$$

$$\Psi_6 = (1/2)\mu_1 + (1/2)\mu_2 + (-1/2)\mu_3 + (-1/2)\mu_4$$

Another way to think of the concept of orthogonality is to consider the total variability of the observed scores, Y. The one-way ANOVA partitions this total variability into two nonoverlapping parts, called "sums of squares," SS_B and SS_W. The partitioning is shown in Figure 1.4, where the circles represent the total variability in Y, called SS_{Total}. Orthogonal comparisons further partition the between variability, SS_B, into $J - 1$ orthogonal parts. Each of these parts is a source of variability associated with one of the $J - 1$ orthogonal comparisons.

The issue of orthogonality is secondary in some situations and unimportant in others. Orthogonality often is associated with planned comparisons. Sometimes the comparisons you plan fit the orthogonality pattern, and then some authors feel that control of α for each comparison is appropriate. If you have this situation, then make the decision to control α in this manner a considered one—don't just follow the herd.

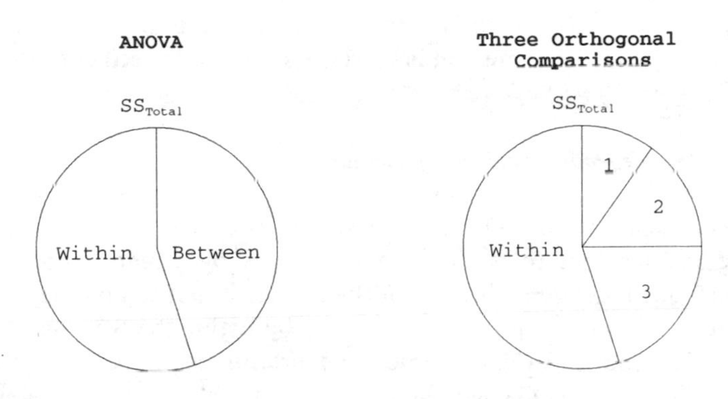

Figure 1.4. Partitioning Total Variability for $J = 4$

The important issues in the area of MCPs are control of α and power. Recognizing that the issue of control of α broadens into the different ways of controlling error rate, ERPC, ERPF, and ERFW, we still need to concentrate on the two topics central to all hypothesis testing: control of α and power.

SAS and SPSS

While many MCPs can be computed simply, without a computer, some of the more recent methods are relatively computer dependent. As you will see in Chapter 2, some methods can be done with a good calculator, but a computer program makes the task easy instead of tedious. Most modern computations of statistics are done with computer programs, and many researchers are generally familiar with such programs.

When multiple comparisons are requested from most packages of statistical programs, such as SAS and SPSS, all possible pairwise comparisons are computed automatically. Other comparisons are available, but often have some restrictions placed on their use, such as a limitation on which MCPs may be selected.

SAS

Within the package of statistical programs called Statistical Analysis System (SAS), you can do pairwise comparisons on J means from either the PROC ANOVA routine or the PROC GLM routine (SAS Institute,

1990). Fifteen different MCPs are available and easily implemented with an optional statement that is used the same way in either of the two PROCs:

MEANS *independent variables/mcp names*;

where *independent variables* are the variables used in the *CLASS* statement as the independent (classification) variables by which subjects are grouped, and *mcp names* is a list of the selected MCPs. You may select as many of the different MCPs as desired by listing the SAS names for the MCPs in the MEANS statement, separating each MCP name with blanks. The MCPs available (and their SAS names) are Dunn/Bonferroni (BON), Duncan (DUNCAN), Dunnett (DUNNETT), Gabriel (GABRIEL), Hochberg's GT2 (GT2), Fisher's LSD (LSD), Ryan's q and F (REGWQ, REGWF), Scheffé (SCHEFFE), Dunn-Šidák (SIDAK), a Studentized maximum modulus method (SMM), Newman-Keuls (SNK), *usual t* (T), Tukey (TUKEY), and Waller (WALLER). Of these, the MCPs that will not be covered in this text are DUNCAN, GABRIEL, REGWF, SIDAK, SMM, and WALLER. Some coverage will be given to GT2, but it will be brief.

Here is an example of the SAS code necessary to run the ANOVA on the responsibility data with three groups and 14 observations per group, without the specific systems lines that are peculiar to each user's system. The code specifies the MCP that SAS calls TUKEY.

```
(system lines)
DATA EXAMPLE;
INPUT GROUP$;
DO I=1 TO 14;
INPUT Y @@;
OUTPUT;
END;
CARDS;
G1_IR
3 4 2 4 1 2 4 2 3 3 2 1 3 2
G2_DR1
3 3 5 3 4 5 3 5 5 4 3 1 4 3
G3_DR2
4 4 3 4 5 4 5 5 3 2 3 3 4 1
```

```
PROC PRINT;
PROC ANOVA;
CLASS GROUP;
MODEL Y=GROUP;
MEANS GROUP/LINES TUKEY;
```

The variable names/values of EXAMPLE, GROUP, I, 14, and Y can be different names/values that you choose. These variable names/values indicate and give a name to, in order, the data set, the independent (classification) variable, the subscript for *Y*, the number of observations per group, and the dependent variable or score for each subject.

The method of input used in this program assumes that the data are organized by groups, with some label for each group on a separate line preceding the data for that group, and that the individual scores are separated by blanks. In the above code, there were three groups labeled G1_IR, G2_DR1, and G3_DR2, each with 14 scores.

As the data are read, for the variable GROUP the program inputs the value of G1_IR, and then for the variable Y the program inputs the values 3, 4, 2, 4, 1, and so on. It then recycles to the DATA statement and starts over for the next value of GROUP, continuing in this fashion until all the data are read.

The PROC ANOVA; statement must be used as it is given, and the variable GROUP in the CLASS, MODEL, and MEANS statements must agree with the name chosen for the independent variable at the input stage. TUKEY is the name of a multiple comparison method (see Chapter 2). Figure 1.5 shows the output from the overall ANOVA.

The model and "group" both have the same values for df, sum of squares, mean square, *F* value, and probability because the model for a one-way ANOVA contains only the one independent variable. When a

```
                              The SAS System
                     Analysis of Variance Procedure
Dependent Variable: Y
Source               DF    Sum of Squares     Mean Square    F Value    Pr > F
Model                 4    3490.48000000    872.62000000      34.14     0.0001
Error                45    1150.10000000     25.55777778
Corrected Total      49    4640.58000000
           R-Square                  C.V.        Root MSE                Y Mean
           0.752165             13.582671       5.0554701           37.22000000

Source               DF          Anova SS     Mean Square    F Value    Pr > F
GROUP                 4    3490.48000000    872.62000000      34.14     0.0001
```

Figure 1.5. SAS Output From PROC ANOVA

```
                          The SAS System

                  Analysis of Variance Procedure

       Tukey's Studentized Range (HSD) Test for Variable: Y

NOTE:   This test controls the type I experimentwise error rate,
        but generally has a higher type II error rate than REGWQ

                 Alpha=0.05  df=39  MSE= 1.23601
            Critical Value of Studentized Range= 3.445
              Minimum Significant Difference= 1.0223

Means with the same letter are not significantly different.

        Tukey Grouping            Mean       N  GROUP

                     A          3.6429      14  G2_DR1
                     A
               B     A          3.5714      14  G3_DR2
               B
               B                2.5714      14  G1_IR
```

Figure 1.6. SAS Output for TUKEY

two-way ANOVA is done on SAS, the listing under "source" at the bottom of the output contains all of the sources in the model.

The SAS output of MCP results is presented using a vertical "lines" approach, in which any means included in the same line are not significantly different (see Figure 1.6). The means are arranged in order vertically, and the lines are given to the left of the means and are "drawn" with letters. So all of the means included in the A line are not significantly different, same for the B line, and so on. Another output characteristic worthy of mention is that SAS prints the critical value of each MCP but does not warn the user about the different statistics used. That is, the critical values printed by SAS are not comparable because SAS does not use the same statistic for all MCPs. The Tukey MCP was computed to show the output format used by SAS for MCPs. Figure 1.6 shows the next page of output, giving the Tukey results as done by SAS, including the "lines" approach to denoting significance.

Think of the A's and B's as forming two vertical lines, showing means that are not significantly different. The A line includes the DR1 and DR2 groups and the B line shows a cluster of similar means, including DR2 and IR. To see which means are significantly different, find those pairs of means that do not share a common letter. For these data, the DR1 mean differs significantly from the IR mean. There are no other significant differences.

SPSS

Within the package of statistical programs called Statistical Package for the Social Sciences (SPSS), you may compute pairwise comparisons on J means using the ONEWAY command with the RANGES subcommand (SPSS, 1990). The MCPs available (and their SPSS names) are LSD (LSD), Duncan (DUNCAN), Newman-Keuls (SNK), Tukey (both Tukey [a], TUKEY, and [b], TUKEYB; see Chapter 2), a modified LSD (LSDMOD), and Scheffé (SCHEFFE). You can also specify ranges, and thus do any MCP for which critical values can be obtained and that uses the same logic as provided by SPSS.

Here is an example of the SPSS code necessary to run the ANOVA on the responsibility data with three groups and 14 observations per group, without the specific systems lines that are peculiar to each user's system. The code specifies the MCP that SPSS calls TUKEY.

```
(system lines)
SET WIDTH 80
DATA LIST FREE/GROUP Y
BEGIN DATA
1 3 1 4 1 2 1 4 1 1 1 2 1 4 1 2 1 3 1 3 1 2 1 1 1 3 1 2
2 3 2 3 2 5 2 3 2 4 2 5 2 3 2 5 2 5 2 4 2 3 2 1 2 4 2 3
3 4 3 4 3 3 3 4 3 5 3 4 3 5 3 5 3 3 3 2 3 3 3 3 3 4 3 1
END DATA
VALUE LABELS GROUP 1 'IR' 2 'DR1' 3 'DR2'/
ONEWAY Y BY GROUP (1,3)
/RANGES=TUKEY
FINISH
```

The variable names of GROUP and Y and the value labels of IR, DR1, and DR2 can be different names that you choose. You can select additional MCPs by including more lines of /RANGES=name, where *name* is the name SPSS gives to its MCPs (see the above list). The method of input used in this program assumes that the data are organized with the value of the variable GROUP followed by the value of the variable Y, with blanks separating the values. Thus the "1 3" that starts the first line of data indicates 1 for GROUP and 3 for Y. Other pairs of scores also show the pairing of GROUP with Y. Using the FREE type of format, SPSS inputs all of the pairs of GROUP Y scores between the

```
- - - - - - - - - - - - - - - - - - - - O N E W A Y - - - - - - - - - - - - -

      Variable  Y
   By Variable  GROUP
                                     ANALYSIS OF VARIANCE

                                   SUM OF        MEAN           F       F
        SOURCE           D.F.     SQUARES      SQUARES        RATIO   PROB.

BETWEEN GROUPS             2      10.0476      5.0238        4.0758   .0247
WITHIN GROUPS             39      48.0714      1.2326
TOTAL                     41      58.1190
```

Figure 1.7. SPSS Output for ONEWAY

BEGIN DATA and END DATA statements. VALUE LABELS is used to give a label to the values of GROUP, where 1 is labeled IR, and so on. The (1,3) tells the program that you have one dependent variable

```
- - - - - - - - - - - - - - - - - - - - O N E W A Y - - - - - - - - - - - - -
      Variable  Y
   By Variable  GROUP

MULTIPLE RANGE TEST

TUKEY-HSD PROCEDURE
RANGES FOR THE 0.050 LEVEL -

          3.44   3.44

THE RANGES ABOVE ARE TABLE RANGES.
THE VALUE ACTUALLY COMPARED WITH MEAN(J)-MEAN(I) IS..
        0.7850 * RANGE * DSQRT(1/N(I) + 1/N(J))

    (*) DENOTES PAIRS OF GROUPS SIGNIFICANTLY DIFFERENT AT THE 0.050
LEVEL

                            G G G
                            r r r
                            p p p

      Mean       Group      1 3 2

      2.5714     Grp 1
      3.5714     Grp 3
      3.6429     Grp 2      *

HOMOGENEOUS SUBSETS    (SUBSETS OF GROUPS, WHOSE HIGHEST AND LOWEST MEANS
                        DO NOT DIFFER BY MORE THAN THE SHORTEST
                        SIGNIFICANT RANGE FOR A SUBSET OF THAT SIZE)
SUBSET  1

GROUP         Grp 1          Grp 3
MEAN          2.5714         3.5714
- - - - - - - - - - - - - - - - - - -

SUBSET  2

GROUP         Grp 3          Grp 2
MEAN          3.5714         3.6429
- - - - - - - - - - - - - - - - - - -
```

Figure 1.8. SPSS Output for Tukey

and GROUP has three levels. Note that the variable names in the DATA LIST command and the ONEWAY command must agree.

The SPSS output shown in Figure 1.7 is for the one-way ANOVA from the above code. Because this output is from ONEWAY, it shows the sources as BETWEEN and WITHIN groups.

The Tukey MCP is computed to show the output format used by SPSS, and the results are given in Figure 1.8 for the above code. SPSS uses the idea of homogeneous subsets to cluster together means that are not significantly different. Note that there can be a pair of means incorrectly declared significantly different in the "(*) DENOTES PAIRS OF GROUPS SIGNIFICANTLY DIFFERENT" part of the output, but correctly grouped into a homogeneous subset. Thus, if there is a discrepancy, the homogeneous subsets are correct. For these data, IR and DR2 means cluster as a homogeneous subset, and DR2 and DR1 means cluster as a homogeneous subset. For these data, the DR1 mean differs significantly from the IR mean. There are no other significant differences.

2. MULTIPLE COMPARISON PROCEDURES

Many different multiple comparison procedures are available for the one-way ANOVA. Given that you are using a *t* statistic and have made a decision about control of error rate, the choice of MCP is largely a choice of the critical value and thus the theoretical distribution. Table 2.1 presents a summary of all of the MCPs to be given in this chapter. The columns contain different MCPs and the rows some of the characteristics of MCPs. Refer to Table 2.1 often to review the basic information on all of the given MCPs. Unless otherwise noted, the MCPs in this chapter are appropriate for pairwise comparisons for the one-way design with equal numbers of observations per group. MCPs for unequal *n*'s will be covered in Chapter 4. Also, all of the MCPs in this chapter make the usual ANOVA assumptions of normality, equal variances, and independence.

The sections that follow cover the MCPs shown in Table 2.1. For each MCP, we will examine the critical value, the decision rule, and other characteristics included in the rows of Table 2.1.

An MCP That Controls α Using ERPC: *Usual t*

The *t* statistic for a single comparison, either pairwise or nonpairwise, with equal sample sizes, is given in Chapter 1, Equation 12. When you

TABLE 2.1
Multiple Comparison Procedures

	usual t	*Dunn*	*Tukey*	*Scheffé*	*Ryan*
Critical value	t^{α}_{df}	$t^{\alpha'}_{df}$, where $\alpha' = \alpha/C$	$q^{\alpha}_{J,df}/\sqrt{2}$	$\sqrt{(j-1)F^{\alpha}_{j-1,df}}$	$q^{\alpha_p}_{p,df}/\sqrt{2}$, where $\alpha_p = \alpha$ for $p = J$ and $J - 1$, $\alpha_p = 1 - (1-\alpha)^{p/J}$ for $p \le J - 2$
Error rate (designed)	ERPC	ERPF	ERFW for all pw comparisons	ERFW for all comparisons	ERFW for all pw comparisons
Error rate (actual)	ERPC	ERPF and ERFW	ERFW and ERPF	ERFW and ERPF	ERFW and ERPF
Power	highest	good for small C	≤ power for Ryan for all pw comparisons	good for large C or nonpairwise comparisons	good for all pw comparisons
Problems	large p( )	not good for large C	power may be low for less than all pw comparisons	conservative unless large C or nonpairwise comparisons	stepwise, power may be low for less than all pw comparisons
When to use	when you want large power at expense of high p( )	small C	all pw comparisons	large C or nonpairwise comparisons	all pw comparisons

continued

TABLE 2.1
Continued

	Shaffer-Ryan	*Fisher-Hayter*	*Dunnett*	*Newman-Keuls*	*Protected t*
Critical value	$q^{\alpha}_{J-1,\,\mathrm{df}}/\sqrt{2}$ for $p = J$ $q^{\alpha_p}_{p,\,\mathrm{df}}/\sqrt{2}$, where $\alpha_p = \alpha$ for $p = J - 1$, $\alpha_p = 1 - (1 - \alpha)^{p/J}$ for $p \leq J - 2$ only if overall F is significant	$q^{\alpha}_{J-1,\,\mathrm{df}}/\sqrt{2}$ only if overall F is significant	$D^{\alpha}_{J,\,\mathrm{df}}$ for directional H_0, $D^{\alpha/2}_{J,\,\mathrm{df}}$ for nondirectional H_0	$q^{\alpha}_{p,\,\mathrm{df}}/\sqrt{2}$	t^{α}_{df} only if overall F is significant
Error rate (designed)	ERFW for all pw comparisons	ERFW for all pw comparisons	ERFW for all pw comparisons with control mean	ERFW for all pw comparisons	ERFW for all pw comparisons
Error rate (actual)	ERFW and ERPF	ERFW and ERPF	as designed	for $J > 3$, *not* ERFW or ERPF	for $J > 3$, *not* ERFW or ERPF
Power	good for all pw comparisons	good for all pw comparisons	good	see problems	see problems
Problems	stepwise, power may be low for less than all pw comparisons	stepwise, power may be low for less than all pw comparisons	only to be used as designed	large p( ) for multiple H_0, stepwise	large p( ) for partial or multiple H_0, stepwise
When to use	all pw comparisons	all pw comparisons	as designed	only if $J = 3$	only if $J = 3$

NOTE: C = number of comparisons actually computed; J = number of means; p = stretch size = number of means in stretch; df = $\mathrm{df}_W = N - J$; p( ) = p(at least one Type I error); pw = pairwise.

TABLE 2.2
Values of Mean Differences and t Statistics: Helping Behavior Data ($n = 14$, MSw = 1.232601, denominator = .4196257)

	IR (2.57) vs. DR1 (3.64)	*IR (2.57) vs. DR2 (3.57)*	*DR1 (3.64) vs. DR2 (3.57)*
Mean difference	1.07	1.00	.07
t	2.55	2.38	.17

have pairwise comparisons, the formula simplifies to that given in Chapter 1, Equation 15. For a single comparison, this t statistic has a sampling distribution that is exactly a t distribution with df = $df_W = N - J$ if all of the usual ANOVA assumptions are met. For multiple comparisons, you can choose to control error rate per comparison by setting α' for each comparison at α. That is, the MCP called the *usual t* in this text is given by the decision rule to reject H_0 if

$$|t_{\hat{\Psi}}| \geq t^{\alpha}_{df_W} \qquad (1)$$

and otherwise fail to reject H_0. The critical value is an α-level value from the t distribution (Appendix Table B) with df = $N - J$ for each of the C comparisons. Also, the critical value is for a two-tailed[16] test of the nondirectional hypothesis. If you want to compute confidence intervals, you can use the critical value from the *usual t* in combination with Equation 27 from Chapter 1 to get interval estimates of ψ.

Using the helping behavior example from Chapter 1, the *usual t* is computed on the means of the three groups, where IR stands for indirect responsibility, DR1 for direct responsibility, and DR2 for direct responsibility when calls for help were present. The values of the t statistics are given in Table 2.2.

The critical value for the *usual t* with df = 39 is 2.023, found by interpolating on 1/df with critical values for df = 30 and df = 40 from Appendix Table B (use $\alpha = .05$). Values of the t statistics from Table 2.2 show IR to differ significantly from both DR1 and DR2.

For the *usual t*, error rate is controlled at α for each comparison (ERPC) and the power is the highest of all MCPs. Another advantage of the *usual t* is simplicity in terms of understanding, computing, and obtaining critical values. The one principal disadvantage is that it gives excessive probability of at least one Type I error for any group of comparisons. That is, control of α using ERPC of necessity makes ERPF and ERFW larger than α.

For any group of $C \geq 2$ comparisons, the p(at least one Type I error) will be larger than α, because an α-level critical value is used for each comparison. This is shown by

$$\alpha \leq 1 - (1 - \alpha)^C \leq C\alpha\,. \tag{2}$$

However, note that all of the following characteristics are built into your choice of the *usual t*: controlling α using ERPC, large p(at least one Type I error), and high power. When would you use the *usual t*? When you consciously make the choice that you want high power at the expense of high p(at least one Type I error).

Simultaneous Test Procedures

Simultaneous test procedures (STPs) have this label because they simultaneously control the p(at least one Type I error) using ERFW (or ERPF) for a set of comparisons. They are not done in steps, and have one critical value for all of the comparisons in the set. They are the basic and, sometimes, classic MCPs, and also are among the easiest to understand and explain. Thus they are a logical choice to be the next MCPs discussed. Other MCPs that are more complicated, and that are not STPs, will be covered in later sections.

DUNN

The Dunn MCP is based on use of the t distribution with C comparisons that are planned. Not only do you know the *number* of comparisons before the research is done, you also know *which* comparisons will be computed. Dunn's method controls α simultaneously for some groups of comparisons, and thus maintains low ERPF and ERFW.[17] Also, this method is appropriate for pairwise or nonpairwise comparisons.

Dunn's MCP uses the idea of the division of total α into parts. The simplest application of this idea is to divide α evenly among the C comparisons, by setting the α' for each comparison to $\alpha' = \alpha/C$. Dunn (1961) presented this MCP with the contribution of a table for t with probabilities α' for various values of C and df_W, which is given as Appendix Table D.[18] The decision rule is to reject H_0 if

$$| t_{\hat{\Psi}} | \geq t_{\mathrm{df}_W}^{\alpha'} , \tag{3}$$

otherwise fail to reject H_0. When α is divided evenly into C parts of α', then α' is set as $\alpha' = \alpha/C$.[19] As a result, p(at least one Type I error) $< C\alpha'$ is conservatively bounded by α as shown by

$$C\alpha' = C\frac{\alpha}{C} = \alpha . \tag{4}$$

Note that the division of α and calculation of critical values are automatically done for you by choice of critical values from Table D.

If you desire to compute confidence intervals, you can use a critical value from Dunn in combination with Equation 27 from Chapter 1 to get interval estimates of ψ.

For the helping behavior example, we have $\mathrm{df}_W = 39$, $\alpha = .05$, and $C = 3$ for all possible comparisons on the $J = 3$ means. The critical value from Table D is obtained by interpolating on 1/df and found to be 2.50, rounded to two decimal places, as are the other values in Table D. With the t statistics from Table 2.2, we find only the IR versus DR1 difference to be significant using Dunn.

Finally, note that the Dunn method uses the number of comparisons actually being computed, C, in the selection of critical values. The number of means, J, is not used directly in the choice of critical value. Because of reliance on C, the Dunn method will have relatively good power for small sets of planned comparisons and relatively lower power for large sets of planned comparisons. As other methods are introduced, relative power will be considered by comparing critical values of the MCPs covered up to that point.

TUKEY

The Tukey method is based on the Studentized range distribution and is among the best known and most popular MCPs. Even though the Tukey MCP will use the t statistic, the critical values will come from the Studentized range distribution. Thus you need to divide the q critical value by the square root of 2, $q/\sqrt{2}$, to give compatibility with the t statistic. As presented here, the Tukey method will be appropriate only for pairwise comparisons.

Tukey (1953) presented the MCP that will be referred to by his name in a lengthy mimeographed monograph that may be the most frequently cited unpublished paper in the history of statistics.[20] The Tukey MCP controls α using ERFW for all pairwise comparisons on J means. The Dunn MCP accomplishes ERFW control of α by relying on division of α and use of a t critical value at α'. Unlike the Dunn method, the Tukey MCP accomplishes α-control by using an α-level critical value from the Studentized range distribution for J means.[21] That is, control of α is built into the range critical value at the chosen ERFW α level.

The Tukey MCP is given by the decision rule to reject H_0 if

$$|t_{\hat{\psi}}| \geq \frac{q^{\alpha}_{J,\,df_W}}{\sqrt{2}}, \tag{5}$$

and otherwise fail to reject. The critical values for the Studentized range are given in Appendix Table C. The sub- and superscripts on q in Equation 5 give you values with which to enter Table C: J = the number of means, df_W, and the selected overall α. If you want to compute confidence intervals, you can combine the Tukey critical value with Equation 27 from Chapter 1 to get interval estimates for ψ.

For all possible pairwise comparisons, $C = J(J - 1)/2$, the power for Tukey's method is better than the power for Dunn. However, if you are doing fewer than all possible planned pairwise comparisons, it is possible that Dunn will have better power than Tukey. This potential power advantage is due to Dunn's use of C, and not J, in selection of critical values. Remember, C is the number of comparisons actually computed and J is the number of means. Because the Tukey critical values pay attention only to J and not to C, Tukey has lower power for smaller C.

For example, for $J = 4$ and $n = 6$, there are $J(J - 1)/2 = 6$ pairwise comparisons and $df_W = 20$. For $\alpha = .05$, the q critical value for $J = 4$ and $df_W = 20$ is 3.96 and the Tukey critical value is $q/\sqrt{2} = 3.96\sqrt{2} = 2.80$. If you are doing all six of the pairwise comparisons, then for $C = 6$, $df_W = 20$, and $\alpha = .05$, the critical value for Dunn is 2.93. Thus, for all possible pairwise comparisons, Tukey is more powerful than Dunn because $2.80 < 2.93$. However, if you plan to do only $C = 3$ of the pairwise comparisons, the critical value for Tukey is still 2.80, the same as for all six pairwise comparisons, but is 2.61 for Dunn. So for three pairwise comparisons that are planned, Dunn would be more powerful than Tukey because $2.61 < 2.80$. Again, note that Tukey critical values depend on J, the number of means, but not on C, the number of comparisons actually computed.

For the helping behavior data (means and t's in Table 2.2), the Tukey critical value is found by interpolating on 1/df and rounds to $3.44/\sqrt{2} = 2.44$. As was the case for Dunn's, only the DR1 group is significantly different from the IR group.

SCHEFFÉ

The method due to Scheffé (1953, 1959) is the next STP. Like the Tukey method, the Scheffé MCP has a constant critical value for all comparisons on J means. Unlike the Tukey method, the Scheffé method is appropriate for all possible comparisons, not just the pairwise comparisons. You can do literally infinitely many comparisons with the Scheffé method while maintaining control of p(at least one Type I error) at α using ERFW: pairwise comparisons, nonpairwise comparisons, orthogonal polynomials, and so on.

The decision rule for Scheffé is to reject H_0 if

$$| t_{\hat{\psi}} | > \sqrt{(J-1)F^{\alpha}_{J-1,\, df_W}}\,, \tag{6}$$

otherwise fail to reject. The critical value depends on J, the number of means, rather than C, the number of comparisons actually computed. Note that the F in the right portion of Equation 6 is the α-level critical value of F with numerator degrees of freedom of $J - 1$ and denominator degrees of freedom of df_W, from Appendix Table A. This is the same critical value as used for the overall F test, and not the observed value of F. If you want to compute confidence intervals, you can use the Scheffé critical value in combination with Equation 27 from Chapter 1 to get interval estimates for ψ.

A comparison of critical values shows that Scheffé is conservative relative to other methods. For $\alpha = .05$, $J = 4$, and $df_W = 20$, the F critical value is 3.10. One danger in getting critical values is confusion over the use of $df_B = J - 1$, for Scheffé, for the numerator degrees of freedom, and the number of means parameter, J, for Tukey. The Scheffé critical value is

$$\sqrt{(J-1)F^{\alpha}_{J-1,\, df_W}} = \sqrt{(3)(3.10)} = \sqrt{9.3} = 3.05\,, \tag{7}$$

compared with 2.80 for Tukey and 2.93 for Dunn. For all pairwise comparisons, the Scheffé MCP would be conservative relative to the other methods discussed so far.

For the helping behavior data, the critical value is found by interpolating on 1/df and rounds to $\sqrt{(2)(3.24)} = 2.55$. For these data (see Table 2.2), Scheffé gives the same results as Dunn's and Tukey's MCPs, that only DR1 is significantly different from IR.

For general comparisons, Scheffé may be more powerful. For $J = 4$ means, there are 25 general comparisons: pairwise, one versus the average of two, one versus the average of three, and the average of two versus the average of two others. The $\alpha = .05$ Dunn critical values for $df_W = 20$ for values of C of 25, 20, 15, 10, 9, 8, and 7 are 3.55, 3.46, 3.33, 3.16, 3.11, 3.06, and 3.00, respectively. The Scheffé critical value of 3.05 with $J = 4$ means shows that Scheffé would be more powerful than Dunn if there were eight or more planned general comparisons. Dunn would be more powerful for seven or fewer planned general comparisons. If you had not planned the general comparisons, then of the methods discussed so far in this text, only Scheffé would be appropriate to control α using ERFW, regardless of how many were computed.

Stepwise Methods

Stepwise methods are those that do the tests by employing some sequence of steps, each depending on the ones before it.[22] Most of these methods use step-down logic.[23] Step-down methods start with a test on the largest pairwise difference in ordered means and proceed down to smaller differences. Neither of the step-down procedures can be used to compute confidence intervals.

NEWMAN-KEULS

The MCP due to Newman (1939) and Keuls (1952) cannot be recommended if you want to control ERFW at α, because it can give values of P(at least one Type I error) larger than α. Because it is one of several methods that follow the step-down logic, Newman-Keuls is useful to introduce this logic. First, the J means must be arranged in order from the smallest to the largest. Next, consider the concept of *stretch size*, symbolized by p, for any comparison between two of the ordered means. Stretch size is the number of means in the subset of means indicated by the range of the two ordered means in the comparison. For $J = 4$, a comparison of the largest to the smallest mean has $p = J = 4$. If the smallest mean is compared to the second largest, $p = 3$, and comparison of two adjacent means has $p = 2$. So stretch size, p, ranges between J and 2.

The Newman-Keuls method uses a different q critical value for each stretch size, but keeps α the same for all critical values. Thus, for $J = 4$ if .05 is selected, three different q critical values would be selected, using $\alpha = .05$ for p of 4, 3, and 2. The value of p is used in place of J in selecting q critical values from Appendix Table C.

Now that you know some of the basics of the Newman-Keuls method, consider the step-down logic.

1. First, for stretch size $p = J$, test the comparison of the largest versus the smallest means. If it is significant, reject H_0 and proceed to the comparisons of stretch size $p = J - 1$. If the test on the largest comparison is not significant, retain all hypotheses for comparisons of stretch size $p \leq J$.
2. Next, test the two comparisons of stretch size $p = J - 1$. If either of them is significant, proceed to comparisons of the next smaller stretch size. If a comparison of stretch size $p = J - 1$ is not significant, then retain all hypotheses for comparisons that are contained in that stretch.

For example, for four means in order, if the 1 versus 4 (smallest versus largest, $p = 4$) comparison is significant, then do the comparisons for $p = 3$. If the comparison of 1 versus 3 (smallest versus second largest) is not significant, then the hypotheses for 1 versus 3, 1 versus 2, and 2 versus 3 are retained because these comparisons are contained in the nonsignificant 1 versus 3 stretch. Note that these comparisons are not even tested and that the hypotheses they test are said to be retained by implication.

3. Each comparison down to stretch size two is tested in a similar fashion only if the hypothesis it tests has not been retained by implication.

Another way to consider this step-down logic is to realize that a hypothesis for a comparison can be rejected only if two points are both true: The means in the comparison are not contained in a stretch of a previously retained hypothesis, and the comparison exceeds a critical value.

For Newman-Keuls, the decision rule is to reject H_0 if the means in the comparison are not contained in the stretch of a previously retained hypothesis and if

$$|t_{\hat{\Psi}}| \geq \frac{q^{\alpha}_{p,\,\mathrm{df}_W}}{\sqrt{2}}, \tag{8}$$

and otherwise fail to reject. Note that the critical value from Appendix Table C is a function of stretch size p and not the total number of means, J.

The Newman-Keuls MCP controls error rate somewhere between ERFW and ERPC because it sets α for each stretch size and controls α for each group of p ordered means.[24] Because the critical values are a function of p and are smaller for lower stretch sizes, Newman-Keuls is more powerful than Tukey. Ordinarily, you would compare power between MCPs only if they have similar control of α. But because of the popularity of the Newman-Keuls method and the frequent comparison of it to Tukey, we will consider relative power. Remember, Newman-Keuls does not control α using ERFW.

For example, for $\alpha = .05$, $J = 4$, and $df_W = 20$, the Tukey critical value is $q/\sqrt{2} = 3.96/\sqrt{2} = 2.80$. The Newman-Keuls critical value for $p = J = 4$ is the same as that for Tukey, 2.80. For $p = 3$, Newman-Keuls gives $q/\sqrt{2} = 3.58/\sqrt{2} = 2.53$, and for $p = 2$, $q/\sqrt{2} = 2.95/\sqrt{2} = 2.09$. So for stretch size three and two, Newman-Keuls gives lower critical values than Tukey and subsequently higher power, although at the expense of increased p(at least one Type I error).

For the helping behavior data, the Newman-Keuls critical values are obtained by interpolating on 1/df and are rounded to 2.44 for $p = 3$ and 2.02 for $p = 2$. Unlike the Dunn, Tukey, and Scheffé MCPs, the Newman-Keuls method shows a significant difference between the means for DR2 and IR: $p = 2$ and $t = 2.38$, which is larger than the critical 2.02. Also, as for the other MCPs, DR1 versus IR was significant (see Table 2.2).

Newman-Keuls controls the p(at least one Type I error) at α if the overall null hypothesis of equality of all J means is true. Newman-Keuls does not control p(at least one Type I error) at α if multiple null hypotheses are present, because it controls α for each subset of equal means. If there are, say, M of these multiple null hypotheses, then Newman-Keuls will control p(at least one Type I error) at approximately $M\alpha$. For $J = 4$ and two null hypotheses, p(at least one Type I error) is approximately 2α for Newman-Keuls. Stated another way, if you want to control ERFW at α, the Newman-Keuls MCP allows use of critical values that are too small for stretch sizes $p \leq J - 2$. Note that for two or three groups, you cannot have multiple null hypotheses. Because you cannot determine when multiple null hypotheses are present, the Newman-Keuls MCP should not be used for $J > 3$ if you want to control ERFW at α. It was presented here mainly to introduce step-down logic and to lead to the MCP credited to Ryan.

RYAN (REGWQ)

The Ryan MCP may be considered a modification of the Newman-Keuls method. Because the Newman-Keuls MCP changes the number-of-means parameter for each different stretch size, the critical values decrease as stretch size decreases. For Newman-Keuls, the critical values for stretch sizes $p \leq J - 2$ are too small, allowing more false rejections for these smaller stretches. Of course, the Newman-Keuls problem is due to control of α for each set of p ordered means, rather than for the whole experiment.

Ryan (1960) proposed modifying the α for each stretch size p to

$$\alpha_p = \frac{\alpha}{J/p} = \frac{p\alpha}{J}, \tag{9}$$

where α_p is expressed as a fraction of α. Because the fraction, p/J, decreases as p decreases, α_p decreases as p decreases and the critical values would not be too small for stretch sizes $p \leq J - 2$. Also, the decrease in α_p accomplishes control of p(at least one Type I error) at α.

Ryan's original proposal has been twice modified to improve power without compromise of ERFW control of α. First, Einot and Gabriel (1975) proposed to let

$$\alpha_p = 1 - (1 - \alpha)^{p/J}. \tag{10}$$

Second, Welsch (1977a, 1977b) proposed to let α_p be equal to α for stretch size $p = J - 1$. Because the comparison for the largest stretch size, $p = J$, has $\alpha_p = \alpha$, the Welsch modification extends this to the next largest stretch size. These two modifications and the step-down logic introduced for the Newman-Keuls MCP give the current Ryan (REGWQ) method.[25]

For the Ryan MCP, the decision rule is to reject H_0 if the means in the comparison are not contained in the stretch of a previously retained hypothesis and if

$$|t_{\hat{\psi}}| \geq \frac{q^{\alpha_p}_{p,\,df_W}}{\sqrt{2}}, \tag{11}$$

where

$$\alpha_p = \alpha \qquad \text{for } p = J,\ J-1$$

$$\alpha_p = 1-(1-\alpha)^{p/J} \quad \text{for } p \le J-2\,.$$

The SAS computer package recognizes all of the contributions to the current Ryan method by naming it REGWQ: R for Ryan, EG for Einot and Gabriel, W for Welsch, and Q because it uses the range critical value from Appendix Table C.

A comparison of the critical values of Ryan, Newman-Keuls, and Tukey will show that Ryan is more powerful than Tukey. Ryan is not as powerful as Newman-Keuls, but it will not have the Newman-Keuls problem with lack of ERFW control of α. For $\alpha = .05$, $J = 4$, and $df_W = 20$, Table 2.3 shows all of the critical values for each of the three methods as well as α_p for Newman-Keuls and Ryan. For $p = 2$ for Ryan, $\alpha_p = 1 - (1 - \alpha)^{p/J} = 1 - (1 - .05)^{2/4} = .0253205653$, rounded to .0253. Because .0253 is between .05 and .01, the q critical value for $\alpha = .0253$ must be between the q critical values for .05 and .01. Interpolation on the natural logarithms of the α's gives the closest approximation and the value of $q = 2.41$.

Because for $p = J = 4$ and $p = J - 1 = 3$ the value of $\alpha_p = \alpha = .05$, the Ryan critical values are the same as those for Newman-Keuls. However, for $p = J - 2 = 2$, α_p for Ryan is .0253 rather than .05, and the Ryan critical value is larger than that for Newman-Keuls. This larger critical value enables the Ryan MCP to deal with the problem with multiple null hypotheses. For $J = 4$ ordered means, the only possibility for multiple null hypotheses is for the adjacent pairs of 1,2 and 3,4 to be equal within each pair, but unequal between the pairs. The 1 versus 4 comparison (stretch size $p = 4$) would not be within one of these null sets of means. The stretch size $p = 3$ comparisons of 1 versus 3 and 2 versus 4 also would not be within one of the null sets of means. Thus the critical

TABLE 2.3
q Critical Values

	Tukey	*Newman-Keuls*		*Ryan*	
p	$q/\sqrt{2}$	α_p	$q/\sqrt{2}$	α_p	$q/\sqrt{2}$
4	2.80	.05	2.80	.05	2.80
3	2.80	.05	2.53	.05	2.53
2	2.80	.05	2.09	.0253	2.41

values for these comparisons do not need to be larger. However, the stretch size $p = 2$ comparisons of 1 versus 2 and 3 versus 4 would be contained in the multiple null hypotheses, if they exist. Thus, for $p = 2$, the critical values need to be large enough to protect against Type I errors if the multiple null condition exists.

Because two is the maximum number of multiple null hypotheses that could exist when $J = 4$, then the upper bound of p(at least one Type I error) can be computed as

$$1 - (1 - \alpha_p)^2 = 1 - (1 - .0253205653)^2 = 1 - .95 = .05.$$

The Ryan MCP accomplishes control of α using ERFW, even for the condition of multiple null hypotheses.

Results for Ryan computed on the helping behavior data are the same as for the Newman-Keuls, because for $J = 3$, Ryan and Newman-Keuls tests are identical and give identical results. So IR is significantly different from both DR1 and DR2.

Earlier, you learned that the Dunn MCP has relatively good power for small C, the number of planned comparisons. Also, you saw that Tukey has better power than Dunn when all possible pairwise comparisons are computed. However, if $C < J(J - 1)/2$, then Tukey might not have the best power. Comparing critical values for any given situation will show which is most powerful. Our previously simple idea of the MCP with the smallest critical value giving the highest power is complicated with the Ryan MCP. For a given J, the Ryan method gives different critical values for different p's. Thus comparing Ryan to Dunn might give a cloudy answer to the question, Which is most powerful? For example, for $\alpha = .05$, $J = 4$, and $df_W = 20$, if $C = 3$ planned comparisons are used, then the Dunn critical value is 2.61. This value is lower than the $p = 4$ Ryan critical value of 2.80, but higher than the $p = 3$ and $p = 2$ critical values of 2.53 and 2.41. Thus, for this situation, Dunn is more powerful for the largest stretch size, but Ryan is more powerful for the remaining stretch sizes. However, because Ryan is a step-down MCP, you will not get to the smaller stretches if you do not get significance for the larger stretches.

When conflicting answers such as these are given as to which MCP is most powerful, you must make the choice of method based on which comparison is important to the research. Suppose you predict that the difference between the means of two specific groups will be the largest difference. If this largest difference is crucial to the research, if it is one of three planned comparisons, and if the other conditions are the same as the example, then you would choose Dunn. If, on the other hand, all three of the planned comparisons were of equal importance to the research, then Ryan would be better. Note that comparing critical values gives you the basis for choosing the most powerful MCP, and you must choose before the data are collected.

Protected Tests

The MCPs presented thus far do not need a significant overall *F* test before they are computed. In fact, except for the use of MS_W, you would not even need to run the ANOVA. This section introduces three MCPs in which the actual tests on the comparisons are not computed if the overall *F* test is not significant. None of the protected tests can be used to compute confidence intervals.

PROTECTED *t* TEST (FISHER'S LSD)

Often called the *least significant difference* (LSD), the protected *t* test is a popular MCP usually attributed to Fisher (1935). Its popularity is unfortunate, because it controls p(at least one Type I error) at α using ERFW for the full null hypothesis or if $J = 3$. That is, if all of the J means are equal, or if $J = 3$, then the LSD controls α using ERFW. If $J > 3$ and some inequality exists, then the LSD has α-control closer to ERPC.

The decision rule for LSD has two steps: First, test the overall H_0 with the ANOVA *F*. If the *F* is significant, go on to the second step. If the *F* is not significant, then fail to reject H_0 for all comparisons. The second step is to reject H_0 for a comparison if

$$|t_{\hat{\Psi}}| \geq t^{\alpha}_{df_W}, \tag{12}$$

otherwise fail to reject H_0. The critical value is an α-level value from the *t* distribution (Appendix Table B) with $df = N - J$, as was the case for the *usual t*. This MCP is designed for pairwise and nonpairwise comparisons and does not require equal sample sizes. Comparison of critical values with those of other MCPs is not fruitful, because the first step depends on a significant *F*. The LSD is available on SAS, but is not correctly computed because SAS proceeds to do the *t* tests even if *F* is not significant.

The protected t test is so named because you compute the usual t test (see the first section of this chapter) only if the overall ANOVA F test is significant. Thus the F is seen as "protecting" the usual t tests. The "least significant difference" is due to the fact that the α-level t critical value is the smallest critical value that the t statistic must exceed in order to be significant when only a single comparison is considered.

The first step of the LSD has good power and control of α. However, once you proceed to the second step, α is no longer controlled ERFW for $J > 3$. The second step has no adjustment of α and no step-down logic. All comparisons are compared to the same α-level t critical value. As Miller (1981) has pointed out, "However, when, in fact, the null hypothesis is false and likely to be rejected, the second stage of the LSD gives no increased protection to that part (if any) of the null hypothesis which still remains true" (p. 93). The LSD does not control α for partial null hypotheses or multiple null hypotheses. For example, for $J = 4$, if the first three means are equal but the fourth is larger than the first three, there would be a partial null hypothesis in the three equal means. If the LSD made it past step one with a significant F, then the three equal means would be tested with the very powerful t at the α level. If $\alpha = .05$, for the three equal means, p(at least one Type I error) $\leq 1 - (1 - .05)^3 = .142625$. Thus you could have a resulting p(at least one Type I error)[26] of up to .142625 if you used $\alpha = .05$ for each t test with $J = 4$. Poor α-control leads to the recommendation that the LSD method should not be used. I have discussed it here as background for the other methods requiring a significant F, and to point out its problems in an attempt to convince you not to use it.

SHAFFER-RYAN

Shaffer (1979) introduced a modification to any existing step-down range MCP that does not already require a significant overall F test. Modifying the Ryan method gives the decision rule for the Shaffer-Ryan. There are two steps: First, compute the overall ANOVA F test. If F is significant, proceed to the next step. If F is not significant, then fail to reject H_0 for all comparisons. The second step starts with the decision to reject H_0 for the comparison at stretch size $p = J$ if

$$|t_{\hat{\psi}}| \geq \frac{q^{\alpha}_{J-1,\mathrm{df}_W}}{\sqrt{2}}, \tag{13}$$

and fail to reject otherwise. Note that the critical value for this comparison at the largest stretch size is the same as the critical value for stretch size $p = J - 1$. From this point on, you do the Shaffer-Ryan MCP exactly as the Ryan; that is, reject H_0 if the means in the comparison are not contained in the stretch of a previously retained hypothesis and if

$$|t_{\hat{\Psi}}| \geq \frac{q^{\alpha_p}_{p, \mathrm{df}_W}}{\sqrt{2}}, \tag{14}$$

where

$$\alpha_p = \alpha \qquad \text{for } p = J,\ J - 1$$

$$\alpha_p = 1 - (1 - \alpha)^{p/J} \qquad \text{for } p \leq J - 2,$$

otherwise fail to reject H_0. Critical values from the Studentized range, Appendix Table C, like those for Ryan's MCP, can be obtained by interpolation on the natural logarithms of the α's when necessary. The Shaffer-Ryan method is not available on major statistical packages. Also, as with the LSD, comparison of critical values to determine relative power is difficult due to the first step requiring F to be significant.

For the helping behavior data, the overall F was significant, and Shaffer-Ryan results are the same as for Ryan. The largest comparison, IR versus DR1, has a t of 2.55, which is compared to the $p = 2$ critical value of 2.02, as is the t for the next largest comparison, IR versus DR2, $t = 2.38$. The IR mean is significantly different from both the DR1 and DR2 means.

FISHER-HAYTER

Hayter (1986) proposed a modification of the LSD to control the liberal α of that procedure. Hayter suggested using a q critical value with $J - 1$ as the number-of-means parameter for the comparisons after a significant overall ANOVA F. That is, perform the overall F test and, if it is significant at level α, then reject H_0 if

$$|t_{\hat{\Psi}}| \geq \frac{q^{\alpha}_{J-1, \mathrm{df}_W}}{\sqrt{2}}, \tag{15}$$

and otherwise fail to reject H_0 for the pairwise comparisons. The critical value is from the Studentized range distribution, Appendix Table C. To compute the Fisher-Hayter MCP on the helping behavior data, compare all of the t's to $2.86/\sqrt{2} = 2.02$, the critical value obtained by interpolating on 1/df with $J - 1 = 3 - 1 = 2$ as the number of means. IR is significantly different from both DR1 and DR2.

All Treatments Compared With a Control

DUNNETT

When you are interested in comparing all treatment groups with a control group and want to control α using ERFW, the MCP credited to Dunnett (1955) should be used. With $J - 1$ treatment groups and one control, J is the total number of groups and there are $J - 1$ tests of treatment *versus* control. Without loss of generality, let the last group be the control group. Then the first $J - 1$ means will be compared with the Jth mean. Because these comparisons all include the Jth (control) mean, they will not be orthogonal.

If you are comparing all treatment means to a control mean, the desired inference often is directional, or one-sided. For example, the question is often whether or not the treatments are better than the control. When this is the case, you will use one-tailed critical values. However, sometimes you want to detect if the treatment means are simply different from the control mean, either larger or smaller. For such a nondirectional hypothesis, you will use two-tailed critical values. Critical values for Dunnett will be designated as a D and will be selected using a given level of α, J as the total number of means including the control, and df_W. Both one- and two-tailed critical values when sample sizes are equal are given in Appendix Table E.

With equal sample sizes and the control mean as the Jth mean, the decision rule for the Dunnett MCP is to reject H_0 for a comparison

$$\Psi = \mu_j - \mu_J \tag{16}$$

if

$$|t_{\hat{\Psi}}| \geq D^{\alpha}_{J,\, df_W} \tag{17}$$

for directional inferences. You can make nondirectional inferences by using the absolute value of the t statistic and a two-tailed critical value, $D^{\alpha/2}$, from Table E. If you are interested in confidence intervals, you can combine Dunnett critical values and Equation 27 from Chapter 1 to compute interval estimates of ψ. For the $J - 1$ comparisons of treatment means with a control mean, the Dunnett MCP gives better power than other MCPs that control α using ERFW.

SAS allows you to compute Dunnett for nondirectional inferences with the statement

```
MEANS effect/DUNNETT ('label');
```

where *label* is the name you give to the control group in the SAS data. Directional inferences use

```
MEANS effect/DUNNETTL ('label');
```

if all treatments are expected to be less than control, and

```
MEANS effect/DUNNETTU ('label');
```

if all treatments are expected to be greater than control.

If IR is considered the control group in the helping behavior data, then two-tailed tests use a critical value of 2.29, obtained by interpolating on 1/df. IR is significantly different from both DR1 and DR2.

If sample sizes are unequal, you cannot use Table E, and should refer to Hochberg and Tamhane (1987) for the correct tables.

Summary

The 10 MCPs given in this chapter have included one method that controls α using ERPC (*usual t*), and some that control p(at least one Type I error) at α using ERFW or ERPF (Dunn, Tukey, Scheffé, Ryan, Shaffer-Ryan, Fisher-Hayter, Dunnett). Some other procedures control α somewhere between ERPC and ERFW (Newman-Keuls, LSD). Some traditional MCPs, such as Duncan's, have not been discussed because they do not control α using ERFW or ERPF, nor do they form the basis for one of the MCPs presented in this chapter. Some of the methods presented here are not recommended for use, but have been presented because they form a foundation for other, "good" methods. Newman-Keuls and the LSD serve as the starting points for Ryan, Shaffer-Ryan, and Fisher-Hayter, and thus have been discussed but are not recommended. Further comparisons among the various MCPs will be given in the next chapter, including recommendations on which MCPs to use and when.

3. COMPARISON OF MCPs

When you are confronted with several MCPs from which to choose, you might ask the legitimate question, How do I choose from among these MCPs? This chapter should help you answer that question. First, most of the MCPs presented in Chapter 2 will be compared with respect to their critical values and thus their power. Second, they will be computed on a common data set called the *Miller data.* These two approaches to comparing the MCPs should help ease the selection process.

Critical Values and Power

Comparison of critical values depends upon the use of a common statistic for all MCPs. The sampling distribution of the common statistic can be used to line up the critical values for the different MCPs. Within that sampling distribution of the statistic, say t, different MCPs will have different critical values, and the only difference in the MCPs will be their critical values. The power of these MCPs is then inversely related to their critical values (see Figure 3.1, where $crit_1$ gives higher power). Note that we do not get power estimates for the MCPs, but that we often can rank order them with respect to power by examining their critical values. For nondirectional hypotheses for most statistics and MCPs, a general rule is: The smaller the critical value, the higher the power. For directional hypotheses, you must consider the absolute value of the critical value.

In practice, you make decisions about error rate control, what type of comparisons, and how many, and then choose an MCP based on these decisions. The most frequent use of MCPs is for the set of all possible pairwise comparisons. If this is your situation, and you want to control α using ERFW, then from among those MCPs that accomplish ERFW for all pairwise comparisons, you can choose the MCP with the highest power by finding the one with the smallest critical value. You should do the

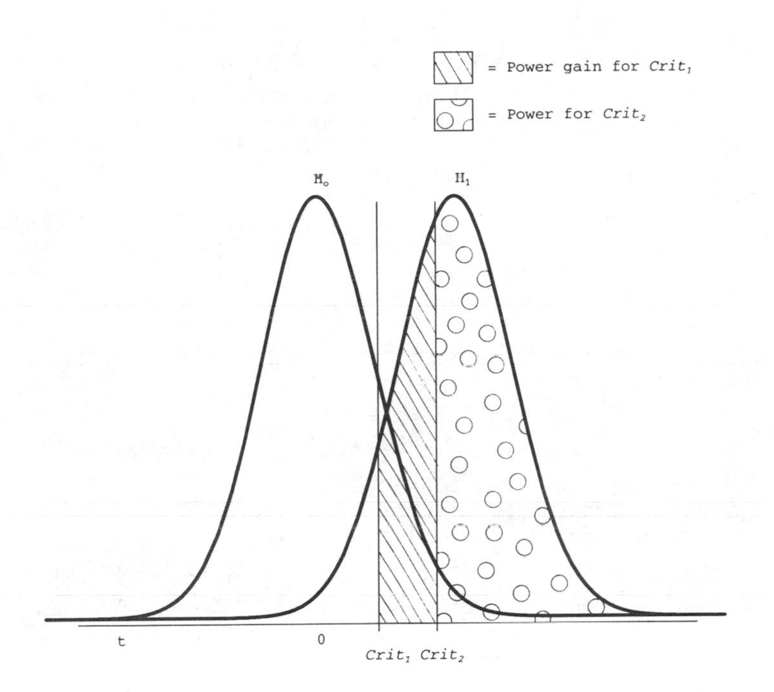

Figure 3.1. MCPs, Critical Values, and Power

comparison of critical values before the start of the data analysis, and not simply run many MCPs and see which one gives the most rejections.

You should restrict your comparison of MCPs to those that give the same error rate control. Of course, you could evaluate critical values for MCPs that offer different control of error rate, such as the *usual t* and Ryan, and the *usual t*, with the smallest critical value, will have the highest power. But this high power is at the expense of excessive Type I errors and an inflated α using ERFW.

Also, note that you could increase power by selecting a value for α larger than .05, say .10 or higher. But if you make this decision, you should make a deliberate, considered choice, and you should use an MCP that has known control of α using ERFW (e.g., Ryan), not an MCP that does not control α using ERFW (e.g., Newman-Keuls). For most MCPs that do not control α using ERFW, the p(at least one Type I error) will vary as a function of either J or the number of null hypotheses,

TABLE 3.1
Critical Values When $J = 5$, dfw = 20, and $\alpha = .05$
With $C = 10$ Pairwise Comparisons

p	*t*	*Dunn*	*Tukey*	*Scheffé*	*Ryan*^{s}	*Shaffer-Ryan*^{s}	*Fisher-Hayter*^{s}	*Newman-Keuls*^{s}	*LSD*^{s}
5	2.086	3.160	2.991	3.388	2.991	2.800*	2.800*	2.991*	2.086*
4	2.086	3.160	2.991	3.388	2.800	2.800	2.800	2.800	2.086
3	2.086	3.160	2.991	3.388	2.765	2.765	2.800	2.531	2.086
2	2.086	3.160	2.991	3.388	2.510	2.510	2.800	2.086	2.086

^{s}Step-down MCP; *requires the overall *F* to be significant.

which will not give you a stable base upon which to build given the choice of a larger α.

Table 3.1 gives critical values for most of the MCPs from Chapter 2 with $J = 5$, $df_W = 20$, and $\alpha = .05$ for all possible pairwise comparisons ($C = 10$). In the table, a superscript s denotes an MCP that uses step-down logic, and an asterisk denotes an MCP that requires the overall *F* to be significant. The *usual t* is included as a benchmark to show the smallest critical value, and highest power, without regard to control of α. Also, Newman-Keuls and LSD are given to show their liberal nature. All critical values are given as *t*, $q/\sqrt{2}$, or $\sqrt{(J-1)F}$.

From Table 3.1, you can order most of the MCPs in terms of power from lowest to highest for those MCPs that control p(at least one Type I error) at α or less using ERFW. The power ranking would be Scheffé (lowest), Dunn, Tukey, Ryan, Fisher-Hayter, and Shaffer-Ryan. Note that the order between Ryan and Fisher-Hayter is not clear. If the overall *F* is significant, the Fisher-Hayter is more powerful for the largest comparison, but for lower stretches Ryan is equally powerful ($p = 4$) or more powerful ($p = 3$ and 2). The *usual t*, Newman-Keuls, and LSD have critical values that are too small for some or all values of *p*, if you want to control α using ERFW.

Next, reconsider Table 3.1 using the same MCPs for $C = 6$ pairwise comparisons that are planned. That is, you did not simply choose the 6 largest comparisons out of the 10 that could be done on 5 means, but planned to do a particular set of 6 pairwise comparisons. Values of *J*, df_W, and α are the same. Only the critical value for Dunn depends on *C*, so this is the only value that is different, 2.93. Consider the Ryan compared with Dunn.

With $C = 6$, Dunn is more powerful for the largest comparison, 2.93 versus 2.991, but Ryan is more powerful for all of the remaining comparisons. If one of the six you planned happens to be the largest comparison, then Dunn will be best for it, but poorer for the rest. Ryan has better power for the smaller stretch sizes. However, if you select Ryan and the largest comparison has a t of, say, 2.95, then the better power for the other comparisons will not be realized because the nonsignificant largest comparison stops the testing.

In this situation, Fisher-Hayter again is unclear with respect to power. If the overall F is significant, then Fisher-Hayter is more powerful than Dunn; if not, then Fisher-Hayter stops testing.

Many more examples could be done to compare power by comparing critical values.[27] To be safe, you should always compare critical values for the common t statistic to find the most powerful MCP for your current research project.

Miller Data

Miller (1981, p. 82) used an example consisting of five means and a value for the standard error of a mean to illustrate many of the MCPs that he presented. This example nicely shows the power differences in many of the MCPs by giving different results for all pairwise comparisons. The data presented in Table 3.2 were simulated to give the values of the means and MS_W computed from the information in Miller (1981). The data are called the *Miller data* and have $J = 5$ groups and $n = 5$ observations per group. Means and variances are given for each group.

The overall analysis shows that there is some significant contrast somewhere among the five group means, but does not show which means are significantly different. Each of the MCPs covered in Chapter 2 will be computed on the Miller data. For those that are available on SAS, output from that package will be given. Table 3.3 contains all possible pairwise mean differences and t statistics.

USUAL t

If you choose to control error rate ERPC, then the *usual t* would be selected as the MCP. You have high power, but at the expense of a large p(at least one Type I error). The SAS output for the Miller data is given in Figure 3.2 for the *usual t*. From this output, the *usual t* shows that the following pairs of means are significantly different: 5-4, 5-3, 5-2,

TABLE 3.2
Miller Data With Group Means (Variances) and ANOVA

	Miller Data				
Group	*One*	*Two*	*Three*	*Four*	*Five*
	18.61	18.86	18.22	22.43	26.32
	13.54	19.17	19.42	17.22	27.01
	16.08	13.69	20.25	22.31	27.08
	18.96	14.47	25.25	19.58	22.32
	13.31	18.81	20.36	23.96	29.77
Mean	16.1	17.0	20.7	21.1	26.5
Variance	7.2044	7.2004	7.2023	7.1943	7.1985

	ANOVA Summary Table				
Source	*df*	*SS*	*MS*	*F*	*p*
Between groups	4	338.84	84.71	11.77	.0001
Within groups	20	144.00	7.20		

5-1, 4-2, 4-1, 3-2, and 3-1. No other MCP will have this many pairs of means significantly different for the Miller data, because not only is the *usual t* most powerful, it does not control p(at least one Type I error) at α. Thus the main question is, Which of these significantly different pairs represent Type I errors?

DUNN AND TUKEY

Because the Dunn MCP is best used when comparisons are planned and C is small, it will be conservative relative to some of the other methods for all pairwise comparisons. However, it will control p(at least one Type I error) at or below the selected α. The Tukey method also

TABLE 3.3
Mean Differences (and t Statistics) for Miller Data

Group	*Two*	*Three*	*Four*	*Five*
One	.9 (0.53)	4.6 (2.71)	5.0 (2.95)	10.4 (6.13)
Two		3.7 (2.18)	4.1 (2.42)	9.5 (5.60)
Three			.4 (0.24)	5.8 (3.42)
Four				5.4 (3.18)

```
                              SAS
                 ANALYSIS OF VARIANCE PROCEDURE

 T TESTS (LSD) FOR VARIABLE: Y
 NOTE: THIS TEST CONTROLS THE TYPE I COMPARISONWISE ERROR RATE,
       NOT THE EXPERIMENTWISE ERROR RATE

            APLHA=0.05  DF=20  MSE=7.20002
            CRITICAL VALUE OF T=2.08596
            LEAST SIGNIFICANT DIFFERENCE=3.54

  MEANS WITH THE SAME LETTER ARE NOT SIGNIFICANTLY DIFFERENT.

       T         GROUPING               MEAN     N  GROUP

                        A             26.500     5  5_FIVE

                        B             21.100     5  4_FOUR
                        B
                        B             20.700     5  3_THREE

                        C             17.000     5  2_TWO
                        C
                        C             16.100     5  1_ONE
```

Figure 3.2. SAS Output, Miller Data, *Usual t*

will control p(at least one Type I error) at α using ERFW, but should be more powerful for all pairwise comparisons than the Dunn. For the Miller data, however, Dunn and Tukey give identical results. SAS output is given in Figure 3.3 for Dunn's method and in Figure 3.4 for Tukey's MCP. For both methods, the significant pairs are 5-4, 5-3, 5-2, and 5-1. Dunn and Tukey show fewer significant pairwise comparisons than the *usual t.*

SCHEFFÉ

For all possible pairwise comparisons, the Scheffé MCP is known to be conservative in terms of both α and power. The SAS results are given in Figure 3.5 for the Scheffé method. Scheffé detects significantly different pairs of means of 5-3, 5-2, and 5-1, but not the 5-4 detected by Tukey and Dunn.

NEWMAN-KEULS

Further coverage of the Newman-Keuls method is given with reluctance due to the fact that it does not control error rate using ERFW. For this reason, this presentation of material on Newman-Keuls will include

```
                        SAS
           ANALYSIS OF VARIANCE PROCEDURE

BONFERRONI (DUNN) T TESTS FOR VARIABLE: Y
NOTE: THIS TEST CONTROLS THE TYPE I EXPERIMENTWISE ERROR RATE
      BUT GENERALLY HAS A HIGHER TYPE II ERROR RATE THAN REGWQ

           ALPHA=0.05  DF=20  MSE=7.20002
           CRITICAL VALUE OF T=3.15340
           MINIMUM SIGNIFICANT DIFFERENCE=5.3515

 MEANS WITH THE SAME LETTER ARE NOT SIGNIFICANTLY DIFFERENT.

      BON       GROUPING             MEAN        N  GROUP

                       A            26.500       5  5_FIVE

                       B            21.100       5  4_FOUR
                       B
                       B            20.700       5  3_THREE
                       B
                       B            17.000       5  2_TWO
                       B
                       B            16.100       5  1_ONE
```

Figure 3.3. SAS Output, Miller Data, Dunn

```
                        SAS
           ANALYSIS OF VARIANCE PROCEDURE

TUKEY'S STUDENTIZED RANGE (HSD) TEST FOR VARIABLE: Y
NOTE: THIS TEST CONTROLS THE TYPE I EXPERIMENTWISE ERROR RATE
      BUT GENERALLY HAS A HIGHER TYPE II ERROR RATE THAN REGWQ

           ALPHA=0.05  DF=20  MSE=7.20002
           CRITICAL VALUE OF STUDENTIZED RANGE=4.232
           MINIMUM SIGNIFICANT DIFFERENCE=5.0782

 MEANS WITH THE SAME LETTER ARE NOT SIGNIFICANTLY DIFFERENT.

         TUKEY GROUPING              MEAN        N  GROUP

                       A            26.500       5  5_FIVE

                       B            21.100       5  4_FOUR
                       B
                       B            20.700       5  3_THREE
                       B
                       B            17.000       5  2_TWO
                       B
                       B            16.100       5  1_ONE
```

Figure 3.4. SAS Output, Miller Data, Tukey

```
                              SAS
                 ANALYSIS OF VARIANCE PROCEDURE

SCHEFFE'S TEST FOR VARIABLE: Y
NOTE: THIS TEST CONTROLS THE TYPE I EXPERIMENTWISE ERROR RATE
      BUT GENERALLY HAS A HIGHER TYPE II ERROR RATE THAN REGWF
      FOR ALL PAIRWISE COMPARISONS

           ALPHA=0.05  DF=20  MSE=7.20002
           CRITICAL VALUE OF F=2.86608
           MINIMUM SIGNIFICANT DIFFERENCE=5.7461

 MEANS WITH THE SAME LETTER ARE NOT SIGNIFICANTLY DIFFERENT.

     SCHEFFE  GROUPING              MEAN     N  GROUP

                   A              26.500     5  5_FIVE
                   A
           B       A              21.100     5  4_FOUR
           B
           B                      20.700     5  3_THREE
           B
           B                      17.000     5  2_TWO
           B
           B                      16.100     5  1_ONE
```

Figure 3.5. SAS Output, Miller Data, Scheffé

notice of its faults and compare it with acceptable methods. In spite of all the bad publicity, however, this method is available on SAS and SPSS and is even popularly used in some applied journals. SAS output is given in Figure 3.6 for the Newman-Keuls method. Newman-Keuls shows that the significantly different pairs of means are 5-4, 5-3, 5-2, 5-1, 4-1, and 3-1.

RYAN

The Ryan MCP should give better power than Tukey for all pairwise comparisons and better α-control than Newman-Keuls. Of course, it is possible for a method to have better power theoretically, but for that elevated power not to appear in the analysis of a given set of data, as was observed for the Tukey method. The SAS output is given in Figure 3.7 for Ryan's method.

The Ryan method shows that the pairs of means that are significantly different are 5-4, 5-3, 5-2, 5-1, and 4-1. For the 3-1 comparison, note that Ryan shows it to be nonsignificant, but Newman-Keuls shows it to be significant. The Newman-Keuls detection of 3-1 as significant is potentially a Type I error.

```
                          SAS
             ANALYSIS OF VARIANCE PROCEDURE

STUDENT-NEWMAN-KEULS TEST FOR VARIABLE: Y
NOTE: THIS TEST CONTROLS THE TYPE I EXPERIMENTWISE ERROR RATE
      UNDER THE COMPLETE NULL HYPOTHESIS BUT NOT UNDER PARTIAL
      NULL HYPOTHESES

            ALPHA=0.05  DF=20  MSE=7.20002

   NUMBER OF MEANS          2          3          4          5
   CRITICAL RANGE     3.54003    4.29353    4.74996    5.07825

 MEANS WITH THE SAME LETTER ARE NOT SIGNIFICANTLY DIFFERENT.

      SNK       GROUPING              MEAN      N  GROUP

                      A             26.500      5  5_FIVE

                      B             21.100      5  4_FOUR
                      B
                      B             20.700      5  3_THREE
                      B
             C        B             17.000      5  2_TWO
             C
             C                      16.100      5  1_ONE
```

Figure 3.6. SAS Output, Miller Data, Newman-Keuls

```
                          SAS
             ANALYSIS OF VARIANCE PROCEDURE

RYAN-EINOT-GABRIEL-WELSCH MULTIPLE RANGE TEST FOR VARIABLE: Y
NOTE: THIS TEST CONTROLS THE TYPE I EXPERIMENTWISE ERROR RATE

            ALPHA=0.05  DF=20  MSE=7.20002

   NUMBER OF MEANS          2          3          4          5
   CRITICAL RANGE     4.27793    4.70315    4.74996    5.07825

 MEANS WITH THE SAME LETTER ARE NOT SIGNIFICANTLY DIFFERENT.

      REGWQ     GROUPING              MEAN      N  GROUP

                      A             26.500      5  5_FIVE

                      B             21.100      5  4_FOUR
                      B
             C        B             20.700      5  3_THREE
             C        B
             C        B             17.000      5  2_TWO
             C
             C                      16.100      5  1_ONE
```

Figure 3.7. SAS Output, Miller Data, Ryan

SHAFFER-RYAN

Because the overall F is significant for the Miller data, proceed to the largest comparison, 5-1, and compare it to the critical value for stretch size $p = J - 1 = 5 - 1 = 4$. Because the t statistic for the 5-1 comparison is $t = (26.5 - 16.1)/\sqrt{[2(7.20002/5)]} - 6.13$, and the critical value for $p = 4$ is $q/\sqrt{2} = 3.96/\sqrt{2} = 2.80$, the 5-1 comparison is significant. The remainder of the comparisons are done exactly as done for Ryan, so 5-4, 5-3, 5-2, 5-1, and 4-1 are significant differences.

FISHER-HAYTER

Because the overall F is significant for the Miller data, the Fisher-Hayter MCP proceeds to compare all t statistics to the $q/\sqrt{2}$ critical value with parameters $J - 1 = 4$ and $df_W = 20$. Because the Fisher-Hayter is not available on SAS, the test must be done using critical values. The critical value for t from Appendix Table C is $3.96/\sqrt{2} = 2.80$. Using t statistics from Table 3.3, the significant differences using Fisher-Hayter are 5-4, 5-3, 5-2, 5-1, and 4-1. Thus, for the Miller data, the Ryan, Shaffer-Ryan, and Fisher-Hayter give the same results and the highest power of the MCPs that control α using ERFW.

DUNNETT

Arbitrarily selecting group one as the control, Dunnett's two-tailed tests showed groups three, four, and five as significantly different from group one (see Figure 3.8) and group two as not significantly different from the control group. Dunnett's one-tailed tests gave the same results.

Summary

Research on MCPs often gives direct comparisons of control of α and power (see Petrinovich & Hardyck, 1969; Ramsey, 1981; Toothaker, 1991). Results from these studies show that many of the MCPs considered in this book are very similar with respect to power for all possible pairwise comparisons. Large differences show up only when these MCPs are compared to methods beyond the scope of this book or on different types of power also not covered here (see Toothaker, 1991). The Fisher-Hayter MCP has not been evaluated in comparative power studies, but might be competitive with these other methods. The Shaffer-Ryan is one of the best MCPs in terms of power.

```
                         The SAS System
                 Analysis of Variance Procedure

               Dunnett's T tests for variable: Y

NOTE: This test controls the Type I experimentwise error for
      comparisons of all treatments against a control.

    Alpha= 0.05  Confidence= 0.95  df= 20  MSE= 7.20002
            Critical Value of Dunnett's T= 2.651
           Minimum Significant Difference= 4.499

Comparisons significant at the 0.05 level are indicated by '***'.

                        Simultaneous             Simultaneous
                            Lower    Difference     Upper
        GROUP            Confidence    Between   Confidence
      Comparison            Limit       Means       Limit

5_FIVE  - 1_ONE             5.901      10.400      14.899    ***
4_FOUR  - 1_ONE             0.501       5.000       9.499    ***
3_THREE - 1_ONE             0.101       4.600       9.099    ***
2_TWO   - 1_ONE            -3.599       0.900       5.399


        Dunnett's One-tailed T tests for variable: Y

NOTE: This test controls the Type I experimentwise error for
      comparisons of all treatments against a control.

    Alpha= 0.05  Confidence= 0.95  df= 20  MSE= 7.20002
            Critical Value of Dunnett's T= 2.304
           Minimum Significant Difference= 3.9107

Comparisons significant at the 0.05 level are indicated by '***'.

                        Simultaneous             Simultaneous
                            Lower    Difference     Upper
        GROUP            Confidence    Between   Confidence
      Comparison            Limit       Means       Limit

5_FIVE  - 1_ONE             6.489      10.400      14.311    ***
4_FOUR  - 1_ONE             1.089       5.000       8.911    ***
3_THREE - 1_ONE             0.689       4.600       8.511    ***
2_TWO   - 1_ONE            -3.011       0.900       4.811
```

Figure 3.8. SAS Output, Miller Data, Dunnett

If availability in commercial statistical packages is important, Ryan would be the best choice. Compared to the best of the most powerful MCPs (Toothaker, 1991), Ryan would lose at most .25 in terms of power. In some cases, Ryan would have better power.

If importance is placed on simplicity, confidence interval computation, or using widely available tables to do the MCP by hand computation, then Tukey would be recommended. Some classroom applications would dictate use of Tukey due to time constraints. The Fisher-Hayter MCP has all of these characteristics except confidence interval computation, and should be more powerful than the Tukey.

Of course, if the research does not demand all possible pairwise comparisons, or does demand some comparisons that are not pairwise but the more general type of comparison, then you must compare critical values to decide which MCP is most powerful for your situation. It is very likely that Dunn can be used in situations where not all possible pairwise comparisons are planned. For the more general comparisons, Scheffé also can be useful.

The bottom-line choice of MCP, if you do all possible pairwise comparisons, have equal sample sizes, have access to computer packages, and want good power and α controlled ERFW, would be the Ryan.

Finally, all of the above results have been obtained with equal sample sizes and all of the ANOVA assumptions met. If any of the assumptions of normality, equal variances, or independence have been violated, or if unequal sample sizes are present, then these recommendations may not hold. Chapter 4 will deal with these issues.

4. VIOLATIONS OF ASSUMPTIONS AND ROBUSTNESS

When you first encounter multiple comparisons, it is natural to consider them as extensions of the ANOVA. Thus it is not surprising to find out that MCPs have the same assumptions as the ANOVA. Of course, the real-world applications of both ANOVA and MCPs do not exactly meet all of these assumptions. That is, it is a very rare case when real data come from normal populations with equal variances and independent observations.[28] When an assumption of a statistic is not met, that assumption is said to be violated. Before you use a statistic, you need to consider the quality of that statistic in the presence of violations of the assumptions; that is, you need to consider the *robustness* of the test. A general definition of robustness to violation of an assumption is that the sampling distribution of the statistic is well fit by the theoretical distribution when the assumption is not met. This fit of the theoretical distribution to the sampling distribution can be examined for either H_0 or H_1.

When an assumption is violated under H_0, the statistic is considered robust to violation of that assumption if α_{true} is approximately equal to α_{set}. That is, we examine "tail" areas of the sampling distribution given H_0, as shown in Figure 4.1.

A statistic is considered robust with respect to power when an assumption is violated and power is still comparable to power when the

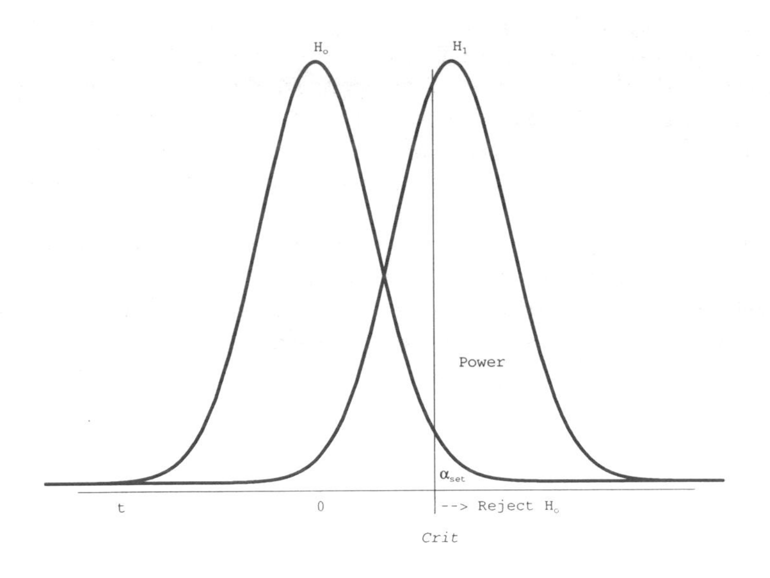

Figure 4.1. α_{set} and Power

assumption is met. That is, we examine areas of the sampling distribution given H_1 that are in the rejection region (see Figure 4.1). Power robustness can also take the form of seeing which of two competitive methods is more powerful when the assumption is violated. Robustness of a statistic must be examined for each assumption.

Of the three ANOVA assumptions, the least likely to be met is normality. Very few of the dependent variables used by applied researchers have normal distributions in the population. In fact, most researchers are not sure of the shape of the distribution, or have not actually given the idea much thought. But if they are asked, most will admit that they do not think the population distribution will be normal in shape. Also, except for extremely large sample sizes, the distribution of the sample data is not a good indicator of the shape of the population. Very nonnormal distributions of sample data can be obtained from normal populations with small to moderate sample sizes. Because of this, the natural question to ask next is, How do MCPs perform if the normality assumption is not met? This question and its answer, for each assumption, constitute the main issue of violations of assumptions and the robustness of MCPs.

The next least likely of the three assumptions is equal population variances. Most treatments that are designed to induce change in some measure of central tendency also change variability, and most likely not in the same way or to the same degree. Even though the sample variances give some picture of the population variances, they are statistics, and any differences may be due to sampling variability as well as true variance differences. So the differences that are present in the sample variances may or may not indicate assumption violation. Then the question is, How do MCPs perform if the equal variance assumption is not met? In the presence of unequal variances, can you still use the MCPs presented in this text?

The assumption most likely to be met is independence. Careful experimental procedures, including randomization of subjects to groups, will likely ensure independence of observations. Two points need to be made regarding independence. First, violations of the independence assumption are usually obvious. For example, subjects worked together in groups, but the dependent variable was an individual score for each subject. Or a study was made of cheating behavior. Or each subject is measured twice. Any process that results in dependent or related scores will give data that violate the independence assumption. Second, if independence is violated for the one-way ANOVA, the bad news is that the effect on α_{true} is dramatic. Research has shown that either the true α is very much larger than the set α, such as $\alpha_{set} = .05$ and $\alpha_{true} = .45$, or it is very much smaller, such as $\alpha_{true} = .001$. The ANOVA F test is not robust to violation of the independence assumption, and MCPs will fit the same pattern. But the good news is that if your research methods include randomization of subjects to groups and if you avoid obvious dependence in the data, the independence assumption of the MCPs will be met.

In the three sections to follow, the traditional MCPs presented in Chapter 2 will be considered for the one-way ANOVA situation with unequal sample sizes and unequal variances, special MCPs for unequal variances will be presented, and robustness to nonnormality of classical MCPs will be covered.

Unequal Sample Sizes and Variances

UNEQUAL SAMPLE SIZES

When you have unequal sample sizes, exact MCPs are difficult to use because of numerical computation problems, except when the number of groups is small (see Hochberg & Tamhane, 1987, p. 91). Also, when sample sizes are unequal, most of the MCPs presented in Chapter 2 cannot be used without modification. Three popular procedures (see Toothaker, 1991) are the Tukey-Kramer procedure (a modification to the *t* statistic to include the unequal *n*'s), the Miller-Winer procedure (a modification to the *t* statistic using the harmonic mean of the unequal *n*'s), and the Hochberg GT2 (a modification using the Tukey-Kramer *t* and a critical value from another distribution called the Studentized maximum modulus). Only the Tukey-Kramer will be presented here.

TUKEY-KRAMER

Because the Tukey method uses the *t* statistic with a common sample size, *n*, you must modify the *t* statistic to use it when sample sizes are not equal. Proposed originally by Tukey (1953) and later independently by Kramer (1956, 1957), the Tukey-Kramer formula for *t* is given as

$$t_{\hat{\Psi}} = \frac{\bar{Y}_j - \bar{Y}_k}{\sqrt{\mathrm{MS_W}\left(\frac{1}{n_j} + \frac{1}{n_k}\right)}}, \qquad (1)$$

where $\mathrm{MS_W}$ is the mean square within from the whole design, but the n_j and n_k are the sample sizes for only the two groups whose means are in the comparison. The Tukey-Kramer procedure follows a decision rule, using the above modified statistic, which is exactly like that for the Tukey: Reject H_0 if

$$|\, t_{\hat{\Psi}} \,| \geq \frac{q^{\alpha_p}_{J,\, \mathrm{df_W}}}{\sqrt{2}} \qquad (2)$$

and otherwise fail to reject H_0. Critical values of q are obtained from Appendix Table C in the same manner as for Tukey. The Tukey-Kramer is simple and maintains control of α using ERFW if variances are equal.

The Tukey-Kramer, Miller-Winer, and Hochberg GT2 were designed to be used with unequal sample sizes, but are appropriate only if the population variances are equal. You may not know if the population variances are equal or unequal for the groups in your study. Thus the typical state of affairs is that you would have to allow for the possibility of unequal variances and consider only statistics that also make this allowance. Simply restated, you should select statistics that are robust to unequal variances.

Unfortunately, the Tukey-Kramer, Miller-Winer, and Hochberg GT2 are not robust to unequal variances, so none of them can be recommended for use unless you strongly believe that the population variances are equal. Evidence for such belief should include approximately equal sample variances and evidence that the sample variances have been similar in previous studies in the research area. Otherwise, when sample sizes are unequal, you should use one of the special MCPs in the next section.

UNEQUAL POPULATION VARIANCES

Because violation of the equal variance assumption is likely to occur in many applied research settings, you need MCPs that are robust to unequal population variances. Two approaches have been taken to this problem: One is to examine the existing MCPs to see if they are robust to unequal variances, and the second is to develop new MCPs that do not depend upon equal variances. These two approaches have to be considered in the context of the equality or inequality of the sample sizes of the groups.

RESEARCH ON OTHER MCPs

The first approach to unequal variances is to examine the performance of the MCPs presented in Chapter 2 when variances are unequal. Most of those methods use equal sample sizes, so our attention needs to be given to their robustness to unequal variances when sample sizes are equal.

First, let us examine the effect on α for the set of all pairwise comparisons. Petrinovich and Hardyck (1969), Keselman and Toothaker (1974), Keselman, Toothaker, and Shooter (1975), and Martin, Toothaker, and Nixon (1989) investigated MCPs with unequal variances. Overall, they found that when n's are equal, the effect of moderately unequal variances (e.g., 1:4 ratio) on the MCPs in Chapter 2 is not severe. If you set $\alpha = .05$, you could choose any one of the methods and use it with little consequence of unequal variances if the maximum true α you would tolerate would be .075. A maximum of .06 would lead to a narrowing of choices to those procedures known to be conservative—Dunn and Scheffé. However, Dunn and Scheffé likely maintain control of α via their conservatism and not by any special robustness, and they do so at the expense of power.

Three notes of caution are needed here. First, these results are for equal n's. Second, these results are for all of the possible pairwise comparisons. Doing fewer than all possible pairwise comparisons might make Dunn more attractive in terms of power. Also, the impact of unequal variances might be higher or lower on specific comparisons than what is shown here for the set of all possible comparisons. Finally, extremely unequal variances might make true α exceed .075.

Now, to see the impact of unequal variances on specific comparisons, we need to consider research done by Games and Howell (1976), who investigated three MCPs when n's were equal and unequal, and when variances were equal and unequal. Two of these procedures were the Tukey-Kramer and a t test that used only the sample variances of the two groups being compared and a $q/\sqrt{2}$ critical value with df $= n_j + n_k - 2$. For all of the pairwise comparisons as a group, these two procedures were liberal or conservative similar to results for the overall ANOVA F. For specific comparisons, using the MS_W in the Tukey-Kramer gave very biased results even in the equal n's case (empirical α's of .010 to .118 even though the overall α was .056). The t with separate variance estimates had less bias for the specific comparisons, but was still poor if both n's and variances were unequal.

Special MCPs

Most of the special MCPs that have been proposed for the unequal variance case (see Keselman, Games, & Rogan, 1979; Tamhane, 1979) also contain unequal sample sizes in the formulas. Research on these MCPs for all possible pairwise comparisons has narrowed the field down to three acceptable procedures: the GH procedure, the C procedure (Dunnett, 1980), and the T3 procedure (Dunnett, 1980; Tamhane, 1979). Only the GH procedure will be given here (see Toothaker, 1991, or the original sources).

THE GH PROCEDURE

Games and Howell (1976) proposed a solution similar to the Welch (1949) approximate solution to the Behrens-Fisher problem.[29] Named GH by researchers since Games and Howell, this MCP uses the statistic

$$t_{jk} = \frac{\bar{Y}_j - \bar{Y}_k}{\sqrt{\dfrac{s_j^2}{n_j} + \dfrac{s_k^2}{n_k}}} \qquad (3)$$

for each pair of means $j \neq k$. The decision is to reject H_0 if

$$|t_{jk}| \geq \frac{q^{\alpha}_{J,\,\mathrm{df}_{jk}}}{\sqrt{2}} \tag{4}$$

and otherwise fail to reject, where

$$\mathrm{df}_{jk} = \frac{(s_j^2/n_j + s_k^2/n_k)^2}{\dfrac{(s_j^2/n_j)^2}{n_j - 1} + \dfrac{(s_k^2/n_k)^2}{n_k - 1}}. \tag{5}$$

Thus you use an α-level critical value from the Studentized range in Appendix Table C with parameters J and df_{jk} as given in Equation 5. A practical suggestion is to round df_{jk} to the nearest whole number to use as the df for the q critical value of the Studentized range in Table C.

Games and Howell (1976) found that the GH procedure maintained α using ERFW close to .05 for equal and unequal variances and equal and unequal sample sizes. GH had a maximum empirical α of .071 for the case of equal variances but unequal sample sizes ($J = 4$, and n's of 6, 10, 14, 16), and .065 or lower for all other conditions. Note that if you believe the population variances are equal, you could use the Tukey-Kramer MCP. For smaller sample sizes, GH gave empirical α's up to .092 for variances of 1, 3, 5, 7 when paired with n's of 11, 8, 4, 3. In their examination of specific comparisons for the effect of unequal variances and/or sample sizes, Games and Howell found that the GH maintained α close to .05. Because it can be liberal with respect to α if sample sizes are small, they recommended use of the GH method if n's are 6 or larger.

Given that GH was only rarely liberal when variances were unequal, and then by only a small amount, and that GH is always more powerful than the C and T3 procedures, GH would be recommended for most applied researchers. Only if it were crucial to maintain strict α-control would you choose C or T3 (see Dunnett, 1980; Tamhane, 1979; Toothaker, 1991).

EXAMPLE

In the example on helping behavior given in Chapter 1, the independent variable was the instructions given to the children and the dependent variable was a rating of helping behavior. Suppose that the

TABLE 4.1
Helping Behavior Example (unequal n's)

	IR (n_1 = 14)	*DR1* (n_2 = 11)	*DR2* (n_3 = 9)
	3	3	4
	2	5	3
	1	4	5
	4	3	5
	3	5	3
	2	3	4
	3	3	4
	4	3	4
	4	5	5
	2	5	
	2	4	
	3		
	1		
	2		
Means (standard deviations)	2.57 (1.02)	3.91 (0.94)	4.11 (0.78)

ANOVA Table

Source	*df*	*SS*	*MS*	*F*	*p*
Between groups	2	17.01	8.50	9.68	.0005
Within groups	31	27.23	0.88		

researcher inadvertently had different numbers of children participate in the instruction conditions, creating unequal sample sizes. Table 4.1 contains data that could have come from such a scenario.

The values for t_{jk}, df_{jk}, and critical values for t with df_{jk} are given in Table 4.2 for the data in Table 4.1. Note that the critical value for $\text{df}_{12} = 22$ had to be interpolated using the rules given in the Appendix. Also note that the critical values are given as t's. The IR mean is significantly different from the means for DR1 and DR2 using the GH procedure, but the DR1 mean is not significantly different from the DR2 mean.

Robustness to Nonnormality of Classical MCPs

When the assumption of normality is violated, there are two basic approaches: Rely upon the robustness of the MCPs presented in Chapter

TABLE 4.2
Values of t_{jk}, df_{jk}, and Critical Values for GH: Helping Behavior Data (unequal *n*'s)

Mean	*IR vs. DR1*	*IR vs. DR2*	*DR1 vs. DR2*
t	−3.40	−4.09	−0.52
df	22	20	18
Critical value	±2.51	±2.53	±2.55

2, or use procedures that do not assume normality. Nonnormality can occur in a variety of ways, but two basic ways are skewness (including outliers in one tail) and kurtosis (including outliers in both tails).[30] Another way to describe distributions is in terms of the length of their tails: A distribution can be short tailed, relative to the normal, such as the uniform distribution, or long tailed, such as the *t*. Several studies have considered the performance of MCPs when sampling from non-normal distributions.

Petrinovich and Hardyck (1969) investigated several MCPs, including Tukey and Scheffé, for an exponential distribution that is positively skewed ($\gamma_1 = 2$, when for a normal distribution $\gamma_1 = 0$) and sharply peaked ($\gamma_2 = 6$, when for a normal distribution $\gamma_2 = 0$). They found little impact of sampling from an exponential distribution except that the power was higher for large differences in means. All MCPs in their study behaved similarly for the exponential distribution.

Keselman and Rogan (1978) studied the Scheffé procedure and Tukey modifications for unequal *n*'s and unequal variances, and included sampling from a chi-square distribution with df = 3 ($\gamma_1 = 1.663$ and $\gamma_2 = 4$). They reported that distribution shape had negligible effect on α.

Dunnett (1982) reported that Tukey is conservative (with respect to both α and power) for long-tailed distributions and for distributions that might also be prone to outliers. Ringland (1983) found that Dunn and a procedure based on the Studentized maximum modulus were liberal for outlier-prone distributions but that Scheffé was conservative. He investigated several robust estimates of location in each of these MCPs and found Scheffé to be robust regardless of situation.[31]

MCPs based on ranks of the observations do not assume normality, but have been found to be very conservative. When their results are compared with those of Scheffé, which is considered the standard of conservatism, the most powerful of the rank methods will reject less often than the

Scheffé method (see Toothaker, 1991). Because of the conservatism of rank tests and the robustness of traditional tests, the traditional MCPs of Chapter 2 are recommended when nonnormality is present.

Finally, a word of caution is offered with respect to a general group of rank tests called *rank transforms* (see, e.g., Conover & Iman, 1981). Concern over the accuracy of these tests has been raised by Sawilowsky, Blair, and Higgins (1989), and you should avoid using MCPs on rank transforms until more information is available.

Summary

If population variances are equal and *n*'s are unequal, use the Tukey-Kramer. However, because you usually cannot be assured that the assumption of equal variances has been met, unequal *n*'s should trigger the use of the MCP called GH, unless it is crucial to maintain strict α-control. With equal *n*'s and unequal variances, only the GH procedure offers α-control for the entire set of comparisons and for individual comparisons. Most MCPs seem to be robust to moderate departures from nonnormality, and the existing rank tests have been found to be conservative or of questionable reputation.

5. MULTIPLE COMPARISONS FOR THE TWO-WAY ANOVA: FACTORIAL OR RANDOMIZED BLOCKS

When the topic of multiple comparisons is covered in most statistics or experimental design texts, considerable attention is placed upon MCPs for a one-way ANOVA, that is, a completely randomized design. Less attention is paid to multiple comparisons in higher-order designs using a two-way or higher ANOVA.[32] Much of the information available from the one-way ANOVA may be extended into the higher-order designs. However, there are some unique problems if you want to use MCPs in higher-order ANOVAs.

There is the overarching problem of complexity: Instead of one *F* ratio, in the two-way ANOVA with more than one observation per cell there are three *F* ratios. In even higher-order ANOVAs, there are more than three *F*'s. Also, in these two-way and higher-order ANOVAs, there are multiple sets of means. There are means for the two main effects, which are the means for the levels of the variables establishing the design, and additionally there are cell means. Multiple comparisons may be needed for each of these three sets of means.

Once you acknowledge that any two-way design leads to greater complexity in the area of multiple comparisons, there are some other important issues that must be considered. Each of these additional issues is tied somewhat to the complexity of the design. First, there is the issue of where α should be controlled: Should you control α for each comparison, for each family of comparisons, or for the entire experiment? Also, there is the issue of cell means versus interaction effects: Which do you want to test?

Example: Study Technique and Cognitive Style

Frank (1984) investigated the effect of two variables on learning from a lecture. He examined study techniques based on note taking and field-independent and -dependent cognitive styles. Subjects were selected from 160 undergraduate female students. The 52 students who scored high (≥ 14) on the Hidden Figures Test (French, Ekstrom, & Price, 1963) were the field-independent group, and the 52 students who scored low (≤ 9) were the field-dependent group. Students in each cognitive style group listened to a taped lecture under one of the following study technique conditions:

1. No notes were allowed (NONOTES).
2. Students were told to take their own notes (STUNOTES).
3. Students were given an outline framework with major headings and subheadings and told to take additional notes on the framework pages (OUTFRAME).
4. Students were given a complete outline with key terms, brief definitions, and important ideas given in addition to the major headings and subheadings and told to take additional notes on the outline pages (COMPOUT).

After a 10-minute review period, students took a 20-item multiple-choice test covering the lecture material. Students had been randomly assigned to one of the four study techniques from within each of the cognitive styles, giving a 2 × 4 randomized block design with 13 observations per cell. Results include data,[33] cell means and standard

TABLE 5.1
Data, Means, Overall *F*'s, Study Technique and Cognitive Style
(n = 13 per cell)

	NONOTES	*STUNOTES*	*OUTFRAME*	*COMPOUT*
FI	13 13 10 16 14	15 19 19 17 19	19 18 17 19 17	15 19 16 17 19
	11 13 13 11 16	17 20 17 18 17	19 17 19 17 15	15 20 16 19 16
	15 16 10	18 18 19	18 17 15	19 19 18
FD	11 14 11 10 15	12 16 16 17 16	18 15 15 14 15	18 19 15 16 19
	10 16 16 17 11	16 16 14 14 16	18 19 18 18 16	18 19 19 18 17
	16 11 10	15 15 15	16 18 16	16 17 15

Cell Means (standard deviations), Row Means, and Column Means

	NONOTES	*STUNOTES*	*OUTFRAME*	*COMPOUT*	
FI	13.15 (2.19)	17.92 (1.32)	17.46 (1.39)	17.54 (1.76)	16.52
FD	12.92 (2.75)	15.23 (1.30)	16.62 (1.61)	17.38 (1.50)	15.54
	13.04	16.58	17.04	17.46	

Overall F's

Source	*df*	*SS*	*MS*	*F*	*p*
COGSTYLE	1	25.01	25.01	7.78	.0064
STUDYTEC	3	320.18	106.73	33.22	.0001
COG × STU	3	27.26	9.09	2.83	.0426
WITHIN	96	308.46	3.21		

deviations (in parentheses) on number of correct items, and the overall *F*'s.[34] All of these are given in Table 5.1.

Even though all three *F*'s are significant, we still have no answers to some of the most interesting questions from this study. Which study technique has the highest mean? Which study technique has the highest mean for field-independent students? For field-dependent students? These questions can best be answered with MCPs.

Control of α

The issue of control of α for a two-way ANOVA has one more level of complexity than the control of α in a one-way design.[35] For a one-way ANOVA, you choose between controlling α for each comparison (ERPC) and controlling α for some family of comparisons (ERPF or ERFW). However, a two-way ANOVA has three families in the experiment. These three families are the two main effects and the cell means (or interaction effects). Thus a new way to control α would be to control error rate for the entire experiment, that is, per experiment or experimentwise.

Even though controlling α per experiment is relatively easy for a two-way ANOVA, it is rarely done by applied researchers. Merely dividing the total α into an $\alpha' = \alpha/3$ for each family will control error rate per experiment, but applied researchers usually make the middle-road choice of controlling α for each of the three families of means. With equal n per cell, comparisons on these three families are mutually orthogonal (orthogonal between the families), and some researchers want to assign α to each family because of this orthogonality. Whatever the reason, the most frequent choice is to control α for each of the three families. When you make this choice, you should realize that the error rate for the whole experiment is approximately three times α.

Main Effect Means

MCPs on the main effect means in a two-way ANOVA are a simple extension of the same MCPs for a one-way ANOVA. That is, you can do Tukey tests on the means for one of the main effects from a two-way ANOVA with very few adjustments to the formulas or concepts used for Tukey on means in a one-way ANOVA.

MCPs ON MAIN EFFECT MEANS

The t statistic for a comparison on main effect means is a simple extension of the t statistic used in the one-way ANOVA. For the A means, the statistic is

$$t_{\hat{\Psi}_A} = \frac{\hat{\Psi} - \Psi}{\sqrt{\frac{MS_W}{nK}\sum_{j=1}^{J} c_j^2}}, \qquad (1)$$

which for pairwise comparisons simplifies to

$$t_{\hat{\Psi}_A} = \frac{\bar{Y}_j - \bar{Y}_{j'}}{\sqrt{\frac{MS_W}{nK}(2)}}, \qquad (2)$$

where the MS_W from the two-way ANOVA is divided by n times K. The value of nK is the number of observations that are summed to compute one of the A means. The use of nK instead of n in the formula for t is the only difference from the same formula for a one-way ANOVA.

For the B means, the statistic is

$$t_{\hat{\Psi}_B} = \frac{\hat{\Psi} - \Psi}{\sqrt{\frac{MS_W}{nJ}\sum_{k=1}^{K} c_k^2}}, \tag{3}$$

which for pairwise comparisons simplifies to

$$t_{\hat{\Psi}_B} = \frac{\overline{Y}_k - \overline{Y}_{k'}}{\sqrt{\frac{MS_W}{nJ}(2)}}, \tag{4}$$

where the MS_W is divided by n times J. Here nJ is the number of observations that are summed to compute one of the B means. The only other difference in the process of doing any of the MCPs on main effect means is to remember that MS_W has $df_W = JK(n - 1) = N - JK$, which is a different formula from that for a one-way ANOVA. Once the t statistic is computed, you can do any of the MCPs covered in Chapter 2 (or Chapter 4) simply by comparing the t to the critical value as given earlier, remembering that df_W has a different formula and that the number of means is J for A means and K for B means. You must also make a choice with respect to how α should be controlled: for the entire experiment, for each of the three families of means, or per comparison.

Now let's do main effect comparisons on the data from the Frank (1984) research. Note that in this example, tests on the main effect may not be of much interest due to some of the original questions and the significant F_{AB}, but we will proceed so we can illustrate main effect comparisons. Using the Tukey method to compare the four means for the main effect of study technique in the example would yield six pairwise comparisons. Controlling α for the family of study technique means, the comparison of means for groups NONOTES and STUNOTES gives

$$t = \frac{16.5769 - 13.0385}{\sqrt{\frac{3.2131}{(13)(2)}(2)}} = 7.1173, \tag{5}$$

which is compared to

$$\frac{q^{\alpha}_{4,60}}{\sqrt{2}} = \frac{3.74}{\sqrt{2}} = 2.64\,. \qquad (6)$$

Because 7.12 is larger than 2.64, the difference in the means for NONOTES and STUNOTES is significant. Similar pairwise comparisons using Tukey show that the means for OUTFRAME and COMPOUT also differ significantly from NONOTES, but no other significant differences exist in the main effect means for study technique. However, you should note that the significant F_{AB} tells us that these results for the main effect may not be true for both levels of cognitive styles. More will be given on this later, in the discussion of cell means tests.

SAS AND SPSS

For main effect means, SAS is easy to use to get MCPs. Simply use the optional statement

MEANS *effects/mcp names;*

where *effects* is one or more of the variables used in the *CLASS* statement as main effects. If tests on main effect means are wanted for both main effects, put the names of both variables in the MEANS statement in place of *effects*, separated by a blank. Also, remember that if you ask for more than one MCP, the MCP names are separated by blanks.

An example is given below of the SAS code necessary to run a two-way ANOVA and compute the Ryan MCP for all possible pairwise comparisons on the means for both main effects. The main effects are called NOTES and FIELD.

```
(systems lines)
DATA EXAMPLE;
INPUT NOTES$ FIELD$;
DO I=1 TO 13;
INPUT TESTSCOR @@;
OUTPUT;
END;
CARDS;
(data)
```

```
PROC PRINT;
PROC ANOVA;
CLASS NOTES FIELD;
MODEL Y=NOTES FIELD NOTES*FIELD;
MEANS NOTES FIELD/REGWQ;
```

The SAS output for MCPs for two-way ANOVAs is the same as that for the one-way ANOVA.

For SPSS, MCPs cannot be done from the command that computes two-way and higher ANOVAs.

Interaction Tests Versus Cell Means Tests

In a two-way ANOVA, there are two approaches for MCPs beyond those done on main effect means: interaction tests and cell means tests (see Games, 1973; Levin & Marascuilo, 1972, 1973; Marascuilo & Levin, 1970, 1976; Rosnow & Rosenthal, 1989). Both approaches will be covered, but I have a preference for cell means tests.

INTERACTION TESTS

The overall test F_{AB} has a hypothesis of no interaction effect, that is, that all $\alpha\beta_{jk}$ are equal to zero. If F_{AB} is significant, it is telling you that not all of the $\alpha\beta_{jk}$ are zero. Tests on interaction effects merely detect which of these $\alpha\beta_{jk}$ are significantly different from each other.[36] Those authors who advocate doing tests on interaction effects properly emphasize that tests on the $\alpha\beta_{jk}$ are the only tests that are directly related to the overall test F_{AB}. Thus tests on $\alpha\beta_{jk}$ have the advantage of direct association with the overall test: The F_{AB} tests for nonzero interaction effects, and the tests on $\alpha\beta_{jk}$ determine whether differences in cell interaction effects are significant.

However, interaction effects are problematic to interpret because they are not the cell means per se, but the effects of the cell means after the main effects have been removed. That is, $\alpha\beta_{jk}$ is the effect of the *jk*th cell mean over and above the main effects, which is shown in the equation for interaction effect:

$$\alpha\beta_{jk} = (\mu_{jk} - \mu) - \alpha_j - \beta_k . \qquad (7)$$

Consider an example given by Rosnow and Rosenthal (1989). The owners of a baseball team want to evaluate a technique designed to improve players'

TABLE 5.2
Ralphing Example

	Means			*Interaction Effects*	
	Ralphing	*Control*	*Average*	*Ralphing*	*Control*
Experienced	7	3	5	.5	–.5
Inexperienced	5	3	4	–.5	.5
Average	6	3	4.5		

ability to deal with the pressures of real competition. This technique is called Ralphing. Experienced and inexperienced players are used and, within each group, are randomly assigned to treatment: Ralphing or control. There are 18 of each type of player and thus 9 players per cell. Performance is number of hits in an experimental game. Table 5.2 gives cell and main effect means and interaction effects for the Ralphing example.

The interaction effects in Table 5.2 will be explained by examining the .5 for the Ralphing and Experienced cell. This .5 is the amount of the effect of the cell mean (7 – 4.5 = 2.5) that is remaining after the main effect of Ralphing (6 – 4.5 = 1.5) and the main effect of Experienced (5 – 4.5 = .5) are removed from the cell mean effect (7 – 4.5 – 1.5 – .5 = 2.5 – 1.5 – .5 = .5). To have a negative quantity, such as –.5, as an "amount remaining" could make interpretation problematic. Any comparison on interaction effects would look at differences; for instance, given Ralphing, the difference in interaction effects for Experienced and Inexperienced is .5 – (–.5) = 1.0.

Rosnow and Rosenthal (1989) chose to talk about the interaction effect in this example by saying "that (in relation to the control) the experienced ball players benefited moderately from Ralphing to the same degree that the inexperienced ball players were harmed by it." But most people would examine the cell means and realize that relative to control, Ralphing helped *both* Experienced and Inexperienced players. The Ralphing and Experienced cell mean is 4 larger than that for Control and Experienced, and the Ralphing and Inexperienced cell mean is 2 larger than that for Control and Inexperienced: Both Experienced and Inexperienced players with Ralphing improved relative to control.

The problem with interpreting interaction effects is that most researchers want to examine all of the effects of a variable, not those remaining after the main effects are taken out. In the terms of the example, what is of interest is the effect of the Ralphing on the players *with their level of experience intact,* not "removed." Expressed another way, most researchers want to discuss the *total* impact of Ralphing, not separate pieces of Ralphing. Comparisons on the cell means offer an analysis of this total impact.[37]

CELL MEANS TESTS

Tests on cell means do not have direct correspondence to the overall test on interaction effects. In fact, cell mean differences are made up of two or more parts. It is important that you realize that differences in cell means contain differences in interaction effects *plus* differences in at least one main effect. For Experienced players, the Ralphing-Control cell mean difference of 7 – 3 = 4 contains not only the difference in interaction effects (.5 – [–.5] = 1.0) but also the difference in main effect means due to Ralphing (6 – 3 = 3). The cell mean difference of 4 will be tested as a unit in one test for the impact of Ralphing on Experienced players, but you must realize that it contains interaction and main effects.

In spite of this lack of correspondence to F_{AB}, tests on cell means are less of a problem to interpret: The cell mean difference of 4 represents, for Experienced players, the gain for Ralphing compared with control. For Inexperienced players, the mean difference of 2 is the gain for Ralphing compared with control: We need to note that these players were not "harmed" by Ralphing, but were helped by it.

The actual t statistic for comparisons on cell means is given by

$$t_{\hat{\Psi}_{\text{cell means}}} = \frac{\hat{\Psi} - \Psi}{\sqrt{\dfrac{\text{MS}_\text{W}}{n} \sum_{j=1}^{J} \sum_{k=1}^{K} c_{jk}^2}}, \qquad (8)$$

which for pairwise comparisons simplifies to

$$t_{\hat{\Psi}_{\text{cell means}}} = \frac{\bar{Y}_{jk} - \bar{Y}_{j'k'}}{\sqrt{\dfrac{\text{MS}_\text{W}}{n}(2)}}. \qquad (9)$$

If you want to do pairwise comparisons on cell means within a row or column, sometimes called *simple effects comparisons*, then Equation 9 is slightly different:

$$t_{\hat{\Psi}_{\text{simple effects}}} = \frac{\overline{Y}_{jk} - \overline{Y}_{j'k}}{\sqrt{\frac{MS_W}{n}(2)}}, \tag{10}$$

where k is constant for both means if you are doing comparisons on the A means at a given level of B.

Thus I prefer tests on cell means because they are easier to interpret, deal with hypotheses that are closer to the original hypotheses tested by most researchers, and contain the total impact on the subjects of both main effects and interaction. Computation of the t statistic for cell means tests is relatively straightforward, but finding critical values is more difficult.

CRITICAL VALUES FOR CELL MEANS TESTS

The focus of finding critical values for tests on cell means is the *number-of-means* parameter. The number-of-means parameter is one of the values used to find a critical value for Tukey, which will be used as an example.[38] Among the symbols used as sub- or superscripts for the q, the number-of-means parameter was the first subscript and had the value of J for the one-way ANOVA.

Up to this point, the number of means for MCPs in a two-way ANOVA was quite apparent because the comparisons were on main effects. For the A main effect means, the number of means is J; for the B main effect means, the number of means is K. For MCPs on cell means, you are dealing with a total of JK cell means. You could consider doing all possible pairwise comparisons on the JK cell means, but this may not be what you want to do; it may not answer your research question. Looking at these JK means from the simple effects perspective, they are J values of A means at each of the K levels of B, or they are K values of B means at each of the J levels of A. Examine Figure 5.1 for simple effects comparisons on cell means.

Assume for the moment that you want to do the simple effects comparisons because doing so will answer the questions posed by your research. You want to examine all of the pairwise comparisons of the A (or B) means at each of the levels of B (or A), that is, comparisons within a row or column. You probably are not interested in comparisons that vary both levels of A and B at the same time, that is, diagonal comparisons. In doing simple effects comparisons, you will be doing a subset of all possible pairwise comparisons on the JK cell means.

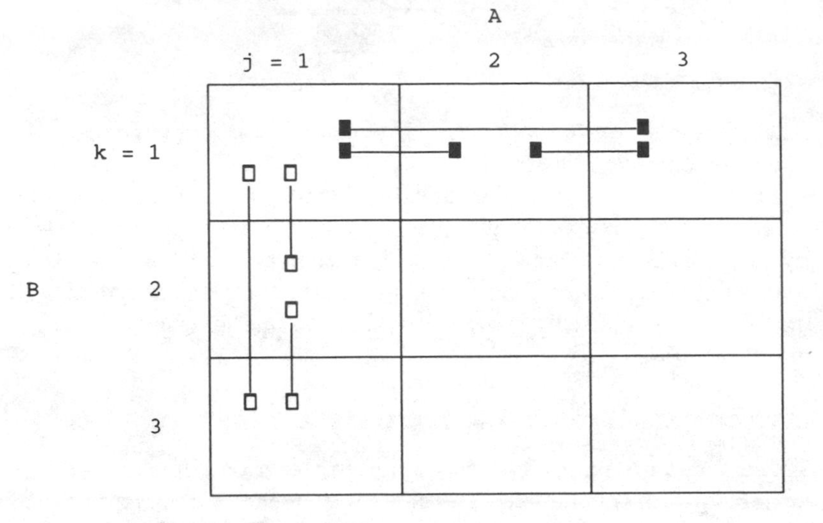

Figure 5.1. Cell Means: Types of Comparisons

■——■ A @ B_1, each A mean at B_1, giving $\frac{J(J-1)}{2}$ comparisons at B_1. Similarly, for each of the K levels of B, yielding $K\left[\frac{J(J-1)}{2}\right] = 3\left[\frac{3(3-1)}{2}\right] = 9$ comparisons total.

□——□ B @ A_1, each B mean at A_1, giving $\frac{K(K-1)}{2}$ comparisons at A_1. Similarly, for each of the J levels of A, yielding $J\left[\frac{K(K-1)}{2}\right] = 3\left[\frac{3(3-1)}{2}\right] = 9$ comparisons total.

Consider three approaches to the number-of-means parameter: two inadequate approaches and one approach appropriate to our research goals. First, using JK as the number-of-means parameter would force you to control α for all $JK(JK-1)/2$ pairwise comparisons. Thus using JK as the number-of-means parameter and doing the simple-effects subset of these comparisons would result in conservative tests.

Second, you could use the number of levels of the appropriate main effect as the number-of-means parameter. For example, if you are interested in A means at each level of B, then J, the number of levels of A, might be considered as the number-of-means parameter. A critical value with J as the number-of-means parameter would control α for one set of the A means, say at B_1, but allow p(at least one Type I error) to increase by α for each set of comparisons. Thus, if you compare the A means at all levels of B, you would have approximately $K\alpha$ for p(at least one Type I error). While using JK gives conservative tests, liberal tests result from using J as the number-of-means parameter (or K, for comparisons on B means at each level of A).

For example, if $J = 4$ and $K = 3$, then $JK = 12$. The simple effects comparisons of the four A means at each level of B would give $J(J - 1)/2 = 4(4 - 1)/2 = 4(3)/2 = 6$ comparisons at each of the three levels of B. Thus, for the $K = 3$ levels of B, there would be $6K = 6(3) = 18$ comparisons of interest. But there are $JK(JK - 1)/2 = 12(12 - 1)/2 = 12(11)/2 = 66$ pairwise comparisons that could be done on the 12 cell means. The 18 comparisons of interest represent a fairly small subset of all 66 possible pairwise comparisons on the 12 cell means. Thus using $JK = 12$ would lead to conservative tests, but $J = 4$ would lead to liberal tests. The ideal value for the number-of-means parameter is somewhere between these two extremes. For $\alpha = .05$, critical values of q with $\text{df}_W = 60$ would be $q = 4.81$ for $JK = 12$ and $q = 3.74$ for $J = 4$, so the ideal value of q lies somewhere between 4.81 and 3.74.

Cicchetti (1972) presents an easy approximate solution to the problem of the number-of-means parameter. Remember that the ideal value of the number-of-means parameter is associated with some number of pairwise comparisons and that the actual number of comparisons being done is known as C. Cicchetti solves the equation

$$C = \frac{J'(J' - 1)}{2} \tag{11}$$

for J' as the approximate number-of-means parameter. In the above example, $C = 18$, so solving for J' gives $18 = J'(J' - 1)/2$ and $36 = J'(J' - 1)$. Possible whole number values for J' are 7, which gives $7(6) = 42$, and 6, which gives $6(5) = 30$. So $J' = 7$ would be the best choice, because $7(6)/2 = 21$ is the closest to $C = 18$ without giving a value of J' that could yield a liberal test.

For tests on A means at each level of B, note that $J' = 7$ as the number-of-means parameter is between $JK = 12$, which would give conservative tests, and $J = 4$, which would give liberal tests. Using $\alpha = .05$, $J' = 7$, and $\text{df}_W = 60$ as the parameters to q in Appendix Table C,[39] the ideal value of q is 4.31, smaller than 4.81 for the conservative tests but larger than 3.74 for the liberal tests.

If you are interested in fewer than all pairwise comparisons on A means or interested in all pairwise comparisons on A means but not for all levels of B, the Cicchetti approach still works for a simple count of the number of comparisons, C. Of course, a similar approach could be taken for tests on the B means at each level of A.

Now let's return to the Frank (1984) research and apply the Cicchetti approach to the example of study technique and cognitive style. We might want to see if there are significant differences in study technique means among the cognitive styles. Because $J(J-1)/2 = 4(4-1)/2 = 6$, there would be six pairwise comparisons of study techniques at FI and six at FD, giving $C = 12$. Using $C = 12$ and solving Equation 11 for J' gives $J' = 6$ as the number-of-means parameter. As an example, using the Tukey method on the comparison of STUNOTES to COMPOUT at FD gives

$$t = \frac{17.3846 - 15.2308}{\sqrt{\frac{3.2131}{13}(2)}} = 3.0634, \tag{12}$$

which is compared to

$$\frac{q^{\alpha}_{6,60}}{\sqrt{2}} = \frac{4.16}{\sqrt{2}} = 2.9416. \tag{13}$$

Because 3.06 is larger than 2.94, the means for STUNOTES and COMPOUT at FD are significantly different, which is unique to field-dependent students. Other significant differences at FD were in agreement with main effect results found earlier: All study techniques perform better than NONOTES. For comparisons on study techniques at FI, significant differences were found for all study techniques compared with NONOTES, but there were no other significant differences. Thus only among field-dependent students do those who take their own notes perform worse than those taking notes with a complete outline. Note that this was not found in the main effect results earlier, nor is it true for field-independent students. This result was found only by examining cell mean differences.

Summary

The problem of complexity of higher-order designs makes the computation of MCPs more involved. You must choose α-control for each comparison, for each family of comparisons, or for the entire experiment. In what is called a two-way ANOVA, most researchers choose to control α for each of the three families of comparisons: the main effect means for A, the main effect means for B, and the cell means. The issue of tests on interaction effects versus tests on cell means has been discussed and resolved in favor of tests on cell means because they are easier to interpret, deal with hypotheses that are closer to the original hypotheses tested by most researchers, and contain the total impact on the subjects of both main effects and interaction. Tests on main effect means are a simple extension of those for the one-way ANOVA. Tests on cell means include finding critical values with the ideal number-of-means parameter using the Cicchetti (1972) approach.

APPENDIX: TABLES OF CRITICAL VALUES

Interpolation Rules

1. Interpolation with respect to df should be done linearly in 1/df.
2. Interpolation with respect to J (or C) should be done linearly in $\log_e J$ (or $\log_e C$).

TABLE A
Critical Values of the *F* Distribution

Degrees of Freedom: Denominator	*Degrees of Freedom: Numerator* 1	2	3	4	5	6	7	8	9	10	11	12	14	16	20
1	161	200	216	225	230	234	237	239	241	242	243	244	245	246	248
	4,052	**4,999**	**5,403**	**5,625**	**5,764**	**5,859**	**5,928**	**5,981**	**6,022**	**6,056**	**6,082**	**6,106**	**6,142**	**6,169**	**6,208**
2	18.51	19.00	19.16	19.25	19.30	19.33	19.36	19.37	19.38	19.39	19.40	19.41	19.42	19.43	19.44
	98.49	**99.00**	**99.17**	**99.25**	**99.30**	**99.33**	**99.34**	**99.36**	**99.38**	**99.40**	**99.41**	**99.42**	**99.43**	**99.44**	**99.45**
3	10.13	9.55	9.28	9.12	9.01	8.94	8.88	8.84	8.81	8.78	8.76	8.74	8.71	8.69	8.66
	34.12	**30.82**	**29.46**	**28.71**	**28.24**	**27.91**	**27.67**	**27.49**	**27.34**	**27.23**	**27.13**	**27.05**	**26.92**	**26.83**	**26.69**
4	7.71	6.94	6.59	6.39	6.26	6.16	6.09	6.04	6.00	5.96	5.93	5.91	5.87	5.84	5.80
	21.20	**18.00**	**16.69**	**15.98**	**15.52**	**15.21**	**14.98**	**14.80**	**14.66**	**14.54**	**14.45**	**14.37**	**14.24**	**14.15**	**14.02**
5	6.61	5.79	5.41	5.19	5.05	4.95	4.88	4.82	4.78	4.74	4.70	4.68	4.64	4.60	4.56
	16.26	**13.27**	**12.06**	**11.39**	**10.97**	**10.67**	**10.45**	**10.27**	**10.15**	**10.05**	**9.96**	**9.89**	**9.77**	**9.68**	**9.55**
6	5.99	5.14	4.76	4.53	4.39	4.28	4.21	4.15	4.10	4.06	4.03	4.00	3.96	3.92	3.87
	13.74	**10.92**	**9.78**	**9.15**	**8.75**	**8.47**	**8.26**	**8.10**	**7.98**	**7.87**	**7.79**	**7.72**	**7.60**	**7.52**	**7.39**
7	5.59	4.47	4.35	4.12	3.97	3.87	3.79	3.73	3.68	3.63	3.60	3.57	3.52	3.49	3.44
	12.25	**9.55**	**8.45**	**7.85**	**7.46**	**7.19**	**7.00**	**6.84**	**6.71**	**6.62**	**6.54**	**6.47**	**6.35**	**6.27**	**6.15**
8	5.32	4.46	4.07	3.84	3.69	3.58	3.50	3.44	3.39	3.34	3.31	3.28	3.23	3.20	3.15
	11.26	**8.65**	**7.59**	**7.01**	**6.63**	**6.37**	**6.19**	**6.03**	**5.91**	**5.82**	**5.74**	**5.67**	**5.56**	**5.48**	**5.36**
9	5.12	4.26	3.86	3.63	3.48	3.37	3.29	3.23	3.18	3.13	3.10	3.07	3.02	2.98	2.93
	10.56	**8.02**	**6.99**	**6.42**	**6.06**	**5.80**	**5.62**	**5.47**	**5.35**	**5.26**	**5.18**	**5.11**	**5.00**	**4.92**	**4.80**
10	4.96	4.10	3.71	3.48	3.33	3.22	3.14	3.07	3.02	2.97	2.94	2.91	2.86	2.82	2.77
	10.04	**7.56**	**6.55**	**5.99**	**5.64**	**5.39**	**5.21**	**5.06**	**4.95**	**4.85**	**4.78**	**4.71**	**4.60**	**4.52**	**4.41**
11	4.84	3.98	3.59	3.36	3.20	3.09	3.01	2.95	2.90	2.86	2.82	2.79	2.74	2.70	2.65
	9.65	**7.20**	**6.22**	**5.67**	**5.32**	**5.07**	**4.88**	**4.74**	**4.63**	**4.54**	**4.46**	**4.40**	**4.29**	**4.21**	**4.10**
12	4.75	3.88	3.49	3.26	3.11	3.00	2.92	2.85	2.80	2.76	2.72	2.69	2.64	2.60	2.54
	9.33	**6.93**	**5.95**	**5.41**	**5.06**	**4.82**	**4.65**	**4.50**	**4.39**	**4.30**	**4.22**	**4.16**	**4.05**	**3.98**	**3.86**
13	4.67	3.80	3.41	3.18	3.02	2.92	2.84	2.77	2.72	2.67	2.63	2.60	2.55	2.51	2.46
	9.07	**6.70**	**5.74**	**5.20**	**4.86**	**4.62**	**4.44**	**4.30**	**4.19**	**4.10**	**4.02**	**3.96**	**3.85**	**3.78**	**3.67**
14	4.60	3.74	3.34	3.11	2.96	2.85	2.77	2.70	2.65	2.60	2.56	2.53	2.48	2.44	2.39
	8.86	**6.51**	**5.56**	**5.03**	**4.69**	**4.46**	**4.28**	**4.14**	**4.03**	**3.94**	**3.86**	**3.80**	**3.70**	**3.62**	**3.51**
15	4.54	3.68	3.29	3.06	2.90	2.79	2.70	2.64	2.59	2.55	2.51	2.48	2.43	2.39	2.33
	8.68	**6.36**	**5.42**	**4.89**	**4.56**	**4.32**	**4.14**	**4.00**	**3.89**	**3.80**	**3.73**	**3.67**	**3.56**	**3.48**	**3.36**
16	4.49	3.63	3.24	3.01	2.85	2.74	2.66	2.59	2.54	2.49	2.45	2.42	2.37	2.33	2.28
	8.53	**6.23**	**5.29**	**4.77**	**4.44**	**4.20**	**4.03**	**3.89**	**3.78**	**3.69**	**3.61**	**3.55**	**3.45**	**3.37**	**3.25**
17	4.45	3.59	3.20	2.96	2.81	2.70	2.62	2.55	2.50	2.45	2.41	2.38	2.33	2.29	2.23
	8.40	**6.11**	**5.18**	**4.67**	**4.34**	**4.10**	**3.93**	**3.79**	**3.68**	**3.59**	**3.52**	**3.45**	**3.35**	**3.27**	**3.16**
18	4.41	3.55	3.16	2.93	2.77	2.66	2.58	2.51	2.46	2.41	2.37	2.34	2.29	2.25	2.19
	8.28	**6.01**	**5.09**	**4.58**	**4.25**	**4.01**	**3.85**	**3.71**	**3.60**	**3.51**	**3.44**	**3.37**	**3.27**	**3.19**	**3.07**
19	4.38	3.52	3.13	2.90	2.74	2.63	2.55	2.48	2.43	2.38	2.34	2.31	2.26	2.21	2.15
	8.18	**5.93**	**5.01**	**4.50**	**4.17**	**3.94**	**3.77**	**3.63**	**3.52**	**3.43**	**3.36**	**3.30**	**3.19**	**3.12**	**3.00**
20	4.35	3.49	3.10	2.87	2.71	2.60	2.52	2.45	2.40	2.35	2.31	2.28	2.23	2.18	2.12
	8.10	**5.85**	**4.94**	**4.43**	**4.10**	**3.87**	**3.71**	**3.56**	**3.45**	**3.37**	**3.30**	**3.23**	**3.13**	**3.05**	**2.94**
21	4.32	3.47	3.07	2.84	2.68	2.57	2.49	2.42	2.37	2.32	2.28	2.25	2.20	2.15	2.09
	8.02	**5.78**	**4.87**	**4.37**	**4.04**	**3.81**	**3.65**	**3.51**	**3.40**	**3.31**	**3.24**	**3.17**	**3.07**	**2.99**	**2.88**
22	4.30	3.44	3.05	2.82	2.66	2.55	2.47	2.40	2.35	2.30	2.26	2.23	2.18	2.13	2.07
	7.94	**5.72**	**4.82**	**4.31**	**3.99**	**3.76**	**3.59**	**3.45**	**3.35**	**3.26**	**3.18**	**3.12**	**3.02**	**2.94**	**2.83**
23	4.28	3.42	3.03	2.80	2.64	2.53	2.45	2.38	2.32	2.28	2.24	2.20	2.14	2.10	2.04
	7.88	**5.66**	**4.76**	**4.26**	**3.94**	**3.71**	**3.54**	**3.41**	**3.30**	**3.21**	**3.14**	**3.07**	**2.97**	**2.89**	**2.78**
24	4.26	3.40	3.01	2.78	2.62	2.51	2.43	2.36	2.30	2.26	2.22	2.18	2.13	2.09	2.02
	7.82	**5.61**	**4.72**	**4.22**	**3.90**	**3.67**	**3.50**	**3.36**	**3.25**	**3.17**	**3.09**	**3.03**	**2.93**	**2.85**	**2.74**
25	4.24	3.38	2.99	2.76	2.60	2.49	2.41	2.34	2.28	2.24	2.20	2.16	2.11	2.06	2.00
	7.77	**5.57**	**4.68**	**4.18**	**3.86**	**3.63**	**3.46**	**3.32**	**3.21**	**3.13**	**3.05**	**2.99**	**2.89**	**2.81**	**2.70**

SOURCE: From *Statistical Methods,* eighth edition, by G. W. Snedecor and W. G. Cochran, copyright © 1989 by the Iowa State University Press, Ames, Iowa, 50010, as adapted by E. W. Minium and R. B. Clarke: *Elements of Statistical Reasoning,* John Wiley & Sons, 1982. Reprinted by permission of John Wiley & Sons, Inc., and Iowa State University Press.

TABLE A
Continued

Degrees of Freedom: Denominator	*Degrees of Freedom: Numerator* 1	2	3	4	5	6	7	8	9	10	11	12	14	16	20
26	4.22	3.37	2.98	2.74	2.59	2.47	2.39	2.32	2.27	2.22	2.18	2.15	2.10	2.05	1.99
	7.72	**5.53**	**4.64**	**4.14**	**3.82**	**3.59**	**3.42**	**3.29**	**3.17**	**3.09**	**3.02**	**2.96**	**2.86**	**2.77**	**2.66**
27	4.21	3.35	2.96	2.73	2.57	2.46	2.37	2.30	2.25	2.20	2.16	2.13	2.08	2.03	1.97
	7.68	**5.49**	**4.60**	**4.11**	**3.79**	**3.56**	**3.39**	**3.26**	**3.14**	**3.06**	**2.98**	**2.93**	**2.83**	**2.74**	**2.63**
28	4.20	3.34	2.95	2.71	2.56	2.44	2.36	2.29	2.24	2.19	2.15	2.12	2.06	2.02	1.96
	7.64	**5.45**	**4.57**	**4.07**	**3.76**	**3.53**	**3.36**	**3.23**	**3.11**	**3.03**	**2.95**	**2.90**	**2.80**	**2.71**	**2.60**
29	4.18	3.33	2.93	2.70	2.54	2.43	2.35	2.28	2.22	2.18	2.14	2.10	2.05	2.00	1.94
	7.60	**5.42**	**4.54**	**4.04**	**3.73**	**3.50**	**3.33**	**3.20**	**3.08**	**3.00**	**2.92**	**2.87**	**2.77**	**2.68**	**2.57**
30	4.17	3.32	2.92	2.69	2.53	2.42	2.34	2.27	2.21	2.16	2.12	2.09	2.04	1.99	1.93
	7.56	**5.39**	**4.51**	**4.02**	**3.70**	**3.47**	**3.30**	**3.17**	**3.06**	**2.98**	**2.90**	**2.84**	**2.74**	**2.66**	**2.55**
32	4.15	3.30	2.90	2.67	2.51	2.40	2.32	2.25	2.19	2.14	2.10	2.07	2.02	1.97	1.91
	7.50	**5.34**	**4.46**	**3.97**	**3.66**	**3.42**	**3.25**	**3.12**	**3.01**	**2.94**	**2.86**	**2.80**	**2.70**	**2.62**	**2.51**
34	4.13	3.28	2.88	2.65	2.49	2.38	2.30	2.23	2.17	2.12	2.08	2.05	2.00	1.95	1.89
	7.44	**5.29**	**4.42**	**3.93**	**3.61**	**3.38**	**3.21**	**3.08**	**2.97**	**2.89**	**2.82**	**2.76**	**2.66**	**2.58**	**2.47**
36	4.11	3.26	2.86	2.63	2.48	2.36	2.28	2.21	2.15	2.10	2.06	2.03	1.98	1.93	1.87
	7.39	**5.25**	**4.38**	**3.89**	**3.58**	**3.35**	**3.18**	**3.04**	**2.94**	**2.86**	**2.78**	**2.72**	**2.62**	**2.54**	**2.43**
38	4.10	3.25	2.85	2.62	2.46	2.35	2.26	2.19	2.14	2.09	2.05	2.02	1.96	1.92	1.85
	7.35	**5.21**	**4.34**	**3.86**	**3.54**	**3.32**	**3.15**	**3.02**	**2.91**	**2.82**	**2.75**	**2.69**	**2.59**	**2.51**	**2.40**
40	4.08	3.23	2.84	2.61	2.45	2.34	2.25	2.18	2.12	2.07	2.04	2.00	1.95	1.90	1.84
	7.31	**5.18**	**4.31**	**3.83**	**3.51**	**3.29**	**3.12**	**2.99**	**2.88**	**2.80**	**2.73**	**2.66**	**2.56**	**2.49**	**2.37**
42	4.07	3.22	2.83	2.59	2.44	2.32	2.24	2.17	2.11	2.06	2.02	1.99	1.94	1.89	1.82
	7.27	**5.15**	**4.29**	**3.80**	**3.49**	**3.26**	**3.10**	**2.96**	**2.86**	**2.77**	**2.70**	**2.64**	**2.54**	**2.46**	**2.35**
44	4.06	3.21	2.82	2.58	2.43	2.31	2.23	2.16	2.10	2.05	2.01	1.98	1.92	1.88	1.81
	7.24	**5.12**	**4.26**	**3.78**	**3.46**	**3.24**	**3.07**	**2.94**	**2.84**	**2.75**	**2.68**	**2.62**	**2.52**	**2.44**	**2.32**
46	4.05	3.20	2.81	2.57	2.42	2.30	2.22	2.14	2.09	2.04	2.00	1.97	1.91	1.87	1.80
	7.21	**5.10**	**4.24**	**3.76**	**3.44**	**3.22**	**3.05**	**2.92**	**2.82**	**2.73**	**2.66**	**2.60**	**2.50**	**2.42**	**2.30**
48	4.04	3.19	2.80	2.56	2.41	2.30	2.21	2.14	2.08	2.03	1.99	1.96	1.90	1.86	1.79
	7.19	**5.08**	**4.22**	**3.74**	**3.42**	**3.20**	**3.04**	**2.90**	**2.80**	**2.71**	**2.64**	**2.58**	**2.48**	**2.40**	**2.28**
50	4.03	3.18	2.79	2.56	2.40	2.29	2.20	2.13	2.07	2.02	1.98	1.95	1.90	1.85	1.78
	7.17	**5.06**	**4.20**	**3.72**	**3.41**	**3.18**	**3.02**	**2.88**	**2.78**	**2.70**	**2.62**	**2.56**	**2.46**	**2.39**	**2.26**
55	4.02	3.17	2.78	2.54	2.38	2.27	2.18	2.11	2.05	2.00	1.97	1.93	1.88	1.83	1.76
	7.12	**5.01**	**4.16**	**3.68**	**3.37**	**3.15**	**2.98**	**2.85**	**2.75**	**2.66**	**2.59**	**2.53**	**2.43**	**2.35**	**2.23**
60	4.00	3.15	2.76	2.52	2.37	2.25	2.17	2.10	2.04	1.99	1.95	1.92	1.86	1.81	1.75
	7.08	**4.98**	**4.13**	**3.65**	**3.34**	**3.12**	**2.95**	**2.82**	**2.72**	**2.63**	**2.56**	**2.50**	**2.40**	**2.32**	**2.20**
65	3.99	3.14	2.75	2.51	2.36	2.24	2.15	2.08	2.02	1.98	1.94	1.90	1.85	1.80	1.73
	7.04	**4.95**	**4.10**	**3.62**	**3.31**	**3.09**	**2.93**	**2.79**	**2.70**	**2.61**	**2.54**	**2.47**	**2.37**	**2.30**	**2.18**
70	3.98	3.13	2.74	2.50	2.35	2.23	2.14	2.07	2.01	1.97	1.93	1.89	1.84	1.79	1.72
	7.01	**4.92**	**4.08**	**3.60**	**3.29**	**3.07**	**2.91**	**2.77**	**2.67**	**2.59**	**2.51**	**2.45**	**2.35**	**2.28**	**2.15**
80	3.96	3.11	2.72	2.48	2.33	2.21	2.12	2.05	1.99	1.95	1.91	1.88	1.82	1.77	1.70
	6.96	**4.88**	**4.04**	**3.56**	**3.25**	**3.04**	**2.87**	**2.74**	**2.64**	**2.55**	**2.48**	**2.41**	**2.32**	**2.24**	**2.11**
100	3.94	3.09	2.70	2.46	2.30	2.19	2.10	2.03	1.97	1.92	1.88	1.85	1.79	1.75	1.68
	6.90	**4.82**	**3.98**	**3.51**	**3.20**	**2.99**	**2.82**	**2.69**	**2.59**	**2.51**	**2.43**	**2.36**	**2.26**	**2.19**	**2.06**
125	3.92	3.07	2.68	2.44	2.29	2.17	2.08	2.01	1.95	1.90	1.86	1.83	1.77	1.72	1.65
	6.84	**4.78**	**3.94**	**3.47**	**3.17**	**2.95**	**2.79**	**2.65**	**2.56**	**2.47**	**2.40**	**2.33**	**2.23**	**2.15**	**2.03**
150	3.91	3.06	2.67	2.43	2.27	2.16	2.07	2.00	1.94	1.89	1.85	1.82	1.76	1.71	1.64
	6.81	**4.75**	**3.91**	**3.44**	**3.14**	**2.92**	**2.76**	**2.62**	**2.53**	**2.44**	**2.37**	**2.30**	**2.20**	**2.12**	**2.00**
200	3.89	3.04	2.65	2.41	2.26	2.14	2.05	1.98	1.92	1.87	1.83	1.80	1.74	1.69	1.62
	6.76	**4.71**	**3.88**	**3.41**	**3.11**	**2.90**	**2.73**	**2.60**	**2.50**	**2.41**	**2.34**	**2.28**	**2.17**	**2.09**	**1.97**
400	3.86	3.02	2.62	2.39	2.23	2.12	2.03	1.96	1.90	1.85	1.81	1.78	1.72	1.67	1.60
	6.70	**4.66**	**3.83**	**3.36**	**3.06**	**2.85**	**2.69**	**2.55**	**2.46**	**2.37**	**2.29**	**2.23**	**2.12**	**2.04**	**1.92**
1000	3.85	3.00	2.61	2.38	2.22	2.10	2.02	1.95	1.89	1.84	1.80	1.76	1.70	1.65	1.58
	6.66	**4.62**	**3.80**	**3.34**	**3.04**	**2.82**	**2.66**	**2.53**	**2.43**	**2.34**	**2.26**	**2.20**	**2.09**	**2.01**	**1.89**
∞	3.84	2.99	2.60	2.37	2.21	2.09	2.01	1.94	1.88	1.83	1.79	1.75	1.69	1.64	1.57
	6.64	**4.60**	**3.78**	**3.32**	**3.02**	**2.80**	**2.64**	**2.51**	**2.41**	**2.32**	**2.24**	**2.18**	**2.07**	**1.99**	**1.87**

NOTE: The values in roman type are for $\alpha = .05$ and those in boldface type are for $\alpha = .01$.

TABLE B

Critical Values of the *t* Distribution

	α for Two-Tailed Test					
	.50	.20	.10	.05	.02	.01
	α for One-Tailed Test					
df	.25	.10	.05	.025	.01	.005
1	1.000	3.078	6.314	12.706	31.821	63.657
2	0.816	1.886	2.920	4.303	6.965	9.925
3	0.765	1.638	2.353	3.182	4.541	5.841
4	0.741	1.533	2.132	2.776	3.747	4.604
5	0.727	1.476	2.015	2.571	3.365	4.032
6	0.718	1.440	1.943	2.447	3.143	3.707
7	0.711	1.415	1.895	2.365	2.998	3.499
8	0.706	1.397	1.860	2.306	2.896	3.355
9	0.703	1.383	1.833	2.262	2.821	3.250
10	0.700	1.372	1.812	2.228	2.764	3.169
11	0.697	1.363	1.796	2.201	2.718	3.106
12	0.695	1.356	1.782	2.179	2.681	3.055
13	0.694	1.350	1.771	2.160	2.650	3.012
14	0.692	1.345	1.761	2.145	2.624	2.977
15	0.691	1.341	1.753	2.132	2.602	2.947
16	0.690	1.337	1.746	2.120	2.583	2.921
17	0.689	1.333	1.740	2.110	2.567	2.898
18	0.688	1.330	1.734	2.101	2.552	2.878
19	0.688	1.328	1.729	2.093	2.539	2.861
20	0.687	1.325	1.725	2.086	2.528	2.845
21	0.686	1.323	1.721	2.080	2.518	2.831
22	0.686	1.321	1.717	2.074	2.508	2.819
23	0.685	1.319	1.714	2.069	2.500	2.807
24	0.685	1.318	1.711	2.064	2.492	2.797
25	0.684	1.316	1.708	2.060	2.485	2.787
26	0.684	1.315	1.706	2.056	2.479	2.779
27	0.684	1.314	1.703	2.052	2.473	2.771
28	0.683	1.313	1.701	2.048	2.467	2.763
29	0.683	1.311	1.699	2.045	2.462	2.756
30	0.683	1.310	1.697	2.042	2.457	2.750
40	0.681	1.303	1.684	2.021	2.423	2.704
60	0.679	1.296	1.671	2.000	2.390	2.660
120	0.677	1.289	1.658	1.980	2.358	2.617
∞	0.674	1.282	1.645	1.960	2.326	2.576

SOURCE: From Table III of Fisher and Yates's *Statistical Tables for Biological, Agricultural and Medical Research,* published by Longman Group UK Ltd, London (previously published by Oliver and Boyd Ltd, Edinburgh), copyright © 1974 by Longman Group UK Ltd, and by permission of the authors and publishers, as adapted by E. W. Minium and R. B. Clarke, *Elements of Statistical Reasoning,* John Wiley & Sons, Inc., 1982. Reprinted by permission of John Wiley & Sons, Inc.

TABLE C
Critical Values of the Studentized Range Distribution

Error df	α	Number of Means (J) or Number of Steps Between Ordered Means: 2	3	4	5	6	7	8	9	10	11
2	.05	6.08	8.33	9.80	10.9	11.7	12.4	13.0	13.5	14.0	14.4
	.01	14.0	19.0	22.3	24.7	26.6	28.2	29.5	30.7	31.7	32.6
3	.05	4.50	5.91	6.82	7.50	8.04	8.48	8.85	9.18	9.46	9.72
	.01	8.26	10.6	12.2	13.3	14.2	15.0	15.6	16.2	16.7	17.8
4	.05	3.93	5.04	5.76	6.29	6.71	7.05	7.35	7.60	7.83	8.03
	.01	6.51	8.12	9.17	9.96	10.6	11.1	11.5	11.9	12.3	12.6
5	.05	3.64	4.60	5.22	5.67	6.03	6.33	6.58	6.80	6.99	7.17
	.01	5.70	6.98	7.80	8.42	8.91	9.32	9.67	9.97	10.24	10.48
6	.05	3.46	4.34	4.90	5.30	5.63	5.90	6.12	6.32	6.49	6.65
	.01	5.24	6.33	7.03	7.56	7.97	8.32	8.61	8.87	9.10	9.30
7	.05	3.34	4.16	4.68	5.06	5.36	5.61	5.82	6.00	6.16	6.30
	.01	4.95	5.92	6.54	7.01	7.37	7.68	7.94	8.17	8.37	8.55
8	.05	3.26	4.04	4.53	4.89	5.17	5.40	5.60	5.77	5.92	6.05
	.01	4.75	5.64	6.20	6.62	6.96	7.24	7.47	7.68	7.86	8.03
9	.05	3.20	3.95	4.41	4.76	5.02	5.24	5.43	5.59	5.74	5.87
	.01	4.60	5.43	5.96	6.35	6.66	6.91	7.13	7.33	7.49	7.65
10	.05	3.15	3.88	4.33	4.65	4.91	5.12	5.30	5.46	5.60	5.72
	.01	4.48	5.27	5.77	6.14	6.43	6.67	6.87	7.05	7.21	7.36
11	.05	3.11	3.82	4.26	4.57	4.82	5.03	5.20	5.35	5.49	5.61
	.01	4.39	5.15	5.62	5.97	6.25	6.48	6.67	6.84	6.99	7.13
12	.05	3.08	3.77	4.20	4.51	4.75	4.95	5.12	5.27	5.39	5.51
	.01	4.32	5.05	5.50	5.84	6.10	6.32	6.51	6.67	6.81	6.94
13	.05	3.06	3.73	4.15	4.45	4.69	4.88	5.05	5.19	5.32	5.43
	.01	4.26	4.96	5.40	5.73	5.98	6.19	6.37	6.53	6.67	6.79
14	.05	3.03	3.70	4.11	4.41	4.64	4.83	4.99	5.13	5.25	5.36
	.01	4.21	4.89	5.32	5.63	5.88	6.08	6.26	6.41	6.54	6.66
15	.05	3.01	3.67	4.08	4.37	4.59	4.78	4.94	5.08	5.20	5.31
	.01	4.17	4.84	5.25	5.56	5.80	5.99	6.16	6.31	6.44	6.55
16	.05	3.00	3.65	4.05	4.33	4.56	4.74	4.90	5.03	5.15	5.26
	.01	4.13	4.79	5.19	5.49	5.72	5.92	6.08	6.22	6.35	6.46
17	.05	2.98	3.63	4.02	4.30	4.52	4.70	4.86	4.99	5.11	5.21
	.01	4.10	4.74	5.14	5.43	5.66	5.85	6.01	6.15	6.27	6.38
18	.05	2.97	3.61	4.00	4.28	4.49	4.67	4.82	4.96	5.07	5.17
	.01	4.07	4.70	5.09	5.38	5.60	5.79	5.94	6.08	6.20	6.31
19	.05	2.96	3.59	3.98	4.25	4.47	4.65	4.79	4.92	5.04	5.14
	.01	4.05	4.67	5.05	5.33	5.55	5.73	5.89	6.02	6.14	6.25
20	.05	2.95	3.58	3.96	4.23	4.45	4.62	4.77	4.90	5.01	5.11
	.01	4.02	4.64	5.02	5.29	5.51	5.69	5.84	5.97	6.09	6.19
24	.05	2.92	3.53	3.90	4.17	4.37	4.54	4.68	4.81	4.92	5.01
	.01	3.96	4.55	4.91	5.17	5.37	5.54	5.69	5.81	5.92	6.02
30	.05	2.89	3.49	3.85	4.10	4.30	4.46	4.60	4.72	4.82	4.92
	.01	3.89	4.45	4.80	5.05	5.24	5.40	5.54	5.65	5.76	5.85
40	.05	2.86	3.44	3.79	4.04	4.23	4.39	4.52	4.63	4.73	4.82
	.01	3.82	4.37	4.70	4.93	5.11	5.26	5.39	5.50	5.60	5.69
60	.05	2.83	3.40	3.74	3.98	4.16	4.31	4.44	4.55	4.65	4.73
	.01	3.76	4.28	4.59	4.82	4.99	5.13	5.25	5.36	5.45	5.53
120	.05	2.80	3.36	3.68	3.92	4.10	4.24	4.36	4.47	4.56	4.64
	.01	3.70	4.20	4.50	4.71	4.87	5.01	5.12	5.21	5.30	5.37
∞	.05	2.77	3.31	3.63	3.86	4.03	4.17	4.29	4.39	4.47	4.55
	.01	3.64	4.12	4.40	4.60	4.76	4.88	4.99	5.08	5.16	5.23

continued

TABLE C
Continued

Number of Means (J) or Number of Steps Between Ordered Means										
12	13	14	15	16	17	18	19	20	α	*Error df*
14.7	15.1	15.4	15.7	15.9	16.1	16.4	16.6	16.8	.05	2
33.4	34.1	34.8	35.4	36.0	36.5	37.0	37.5	37.9	.01	
9.72	10.2	10.3	10.5	10.7	10.8	11.0	11.1	11.2	.05	3
17.5	17.9	18.2	18.5	18.8	19.1	19.3	19.5	19.8	.01	
8.21	8.37	8.52	8.66	8.79	8.91	9.03	9.13	9.23	.05	4
12.8	13.1	13.3	13.5	13.7	13.9	14.1	14.2	14.4	.01	
7.32	7.47	7.60	7.72	7.83	7.93	8.03	8.12	8.21	.05	5
10.70	10.89	11.08	11.24	11.40	11.55	11.68	11.81	11.93	.01	
6.79	6.92	7.03	7.14	7.24	7.34	7.43	7.51	7.59	.05	6
9.48	9.65	9.81	9.95	10.08	10.21	10.32	10.43	10.54	.01	
6.43	6.55	6.66	6.76	6.85	6.94	7.02	7.10	7.17	.05	7
8.71	8.86	9.00	9.12	9.24	9.35	9.46	9.55	9.65	.01	
6.18	6.29	6.39	6.48	6.57	6.65	6.73	6.80	6.87	.05	8
8.18	8.31	8.44	8.55	8.66	8.76	8.85	8.94	9.03	.01	
5.98	6.09	6.19	6.28	6.36	6.44	6.51	6.58	6.64	.05	9
7.78	7.91	8.03	8.13	8.23	8.33	8.41	8.49	8.57	.01	
5.83	5.93	6.03	6.11	6.19	6.27	6.34	6.40	6.47	.05	10
7.49	7.60	7.71	7.81	7.91	7.99	8.08	8.15	8.23	.01	
5.71	5.81	5.90	5.98	6.06	6.13	6.20	6.27	6.33	.05	11
7.25	7.36	7.46	7.56	7.65	7.73	7.81	7.88	7.95	.01	
5.61	5.71	5.80	5.88	5.95	6.02	6.09	6.15	6.21	.05	12
7.06	7.17	7.26	7.36	7.44	7.52	7.59	7.66	7.73	.01	
5.53	5.63	5.71	5.79	5.86	5.93	5.99	6.05	6.11	.05	13
6.90	7.01	7.10	7.19	7.27	7.35	7.42	7.48	7.55	.01	
5.46	5.55	5.64	5.71	5.79	5.85	5.91	5.97	6.03	.05	14
6.77	6.87	6.96	7.05	7.13	7.20	7.27	7.33	7.39	.01	
5.40	5.49	5.57	5.65	5.72	5.78	5.85	5.90	5.96	.05	15
6.66	6.76	6.84	6.93	7.00	7.07	7.14	7.20	7.26	.01	
5.35	5.44	5.52	5.59	5.66	5.73	5.79	5.84	5.90	.05	16
6.56	6.66	6.74	6.82	6.90	6.97	7.03	7.09	7.15	.01	
5.31	5.39	5.47	5.54	5.61	5.67	5.73	5.79	5.84	.05	17
6.48	6.57	6.66	6.73	6.81	6.87	6.94	7.00	7.05	.01	
5.27	5.35	5.43	5.50	5.57	5.63	5.69	5.74	5.79	.05	18
6.41	6.50	6.58	6.65	6.73	6.79	6.85	6.91	6.97	.01	
5.23	5.31	5.39	5.46	5.53	5.59	5.65	5.70	5.75	.05	19
6.34	6.43	6.51	6.58	6.65	6.72	6.78	6.84	6.89	.01	
5.20	5.28	5.36	5.43	5.49	5.55	5.61	5.66	5.71	.05	20
6.28	6.37	6.45	6.52	6.59	6.65	6.71	6.77	6.82	.01	
5.10	5.18	5.25	5.32	5.38	5.44	5.49	5.55	5.59	.05	24
6.11	6.19	6.26	6.33	6.39	6.45	6.51	6.56	6.61	.01	
5.00	5.08	5.15	5.21	5.27	5.33	5.38	5.43	5.47	.05	30
5.93	6.01	6.08	6.14	6.20	6.26	6.31	6.36	6.41	.01	
4.90	4.98	5.04	5.11	5.16	5.22	5.27	5.31	5.36	.05	40
5.76	5.83	5.90	5.96	6.02	6.07	6.12	6.16	6.21	.01	
4.81	4.88	4.94	5.00	5.06	5.11	5.15	5.20	5.24	.05	60
5.60	5.67	5.73	5.78	5.84	5.89	5.93	5.97	6.01	.01	
4.71	4.78	4.84	4.90	4.95	5.00	5.04	5.09	5.13	.05	120
5.44	5.50	5.56	5.61	5.66	5.71	5.75	5.79	5.83	.01	
4.62	4.68	4.74	4.80	4.85	4.89	4.93	4.97	5.01	.05	∞
5.29	5.35	5.40	5.45	5.49	5.54	5.57	5.61	5.65	.01	

SOURCE: From Table 29 in *Biometrika Tables for Statisticians,* Volume 1, second edition, edited by E. S. Pearson and H. O. Hartley, copyright © 1958 by Cambridge University Press, New York, as adapted by R. E. Kirk, *Experimental Design: Procedures for the Behavior Sciences,* second edition, Brooks/Cole Publishing Company, 1982. Reprinted by permission of the Biometrika Trustees and Brooks/Cole Publishing Company, Pacific Grove, CA 93950.

TABLE D

Critical Values for Dunn: Percentage Points of the Dunn Multiple Comparison Test

Number of Compari-sons (C)	α	*Error df* 5	7	10	12	15	20	24	30	40	60	120	∞
2	.05	3.17	2.84	2.64	2.56	2.49	2.42	2.39	2.36	2.33	2.30	2.27	2.24
	.01	4.78	4.03	3.58	3.43	3.29	3.16	3.09	3.03	2.97	2.92	2.86	2.81
3	.05	3.54	3.13	2.87	2.78	2.69	2.61	2.58	2.54	2.50	2.47	2.43	2.39
	.01	5.25	4.36	3.83	3.65	3.48	3.33	3.26	3.19	3.12	3.06	2.99	2.94
4	.05	3.81	3.34	3.04	2.94	2.84	2.75	2.70	2.66	2.62	2.58	2.54	2.50
	.01	5.60	4.59	4.01	3.80	3.62	3.46	3.38	3.30	3.23	3.16	3.09	3.02
5	.05	4.04	3.50	3.17	3.06	2.95	2.85	2.80	2.75	2.71	2.66	2.62	2.58
	.01	5.89	4.78	4.15	3.93	3.74	3.55	3.47	3.39	3.31	3.24	3.16	3.09
6	.05	4.22	3.64	3.28	3.15	3.04	2.93	2.88	2.83	2.78	2.73	2.68	2.64
	.01	6.15	4.95	4.27	4.04	3.82	3.63	3.54	3.46	3.38	3.30	3.22	3.15
7	.05	4.38	3.76	3.37	3.24	3.11	3.00	2.94	2.89	2.84	2.79	2.74	2.69
	.01	6.36	5.09	4.37	4.13	3.90	3.70	3.61	3.52	3.43	3.34	3.27	3.19
8	.05	4.53	3.86	3.45	3.31	3.18	3.06	3.00	2.94	2.89	2.84	2.79	2.74
	.01	6.56	5.21	4.45	4.20	3.97	3.76	3.66	3.57	3.48	3.39	3.31	3.23
9	.05	4.66	3.95	3.52	3.37	3.24	3.11	3.05	2.99	2.93	2.88	2.83	2.77
	.01	6.70	5.31	4.53	4.26	4.02	3.80	3.70	3.61	3.51	3.42	3.34	3.26
10	.05	4.78	4.03	3.58	3.43	3.29	3.16	3.09	3.03	2.97	2.92	2.86	2.81
	.01	6.86	5.40	4.59	4.32	4.07	3.85	3.74	3.65	3.55	3.46	3.37	3.29
15	.05	5.25	4.36	3.83	3.65	3.48	3.33	3.26	3.19	3.12	3.06	2.99	2.94
	.01	7.51	5.79	4.86	4.56	4.29	4.03	3.91	3.80	3.70	3.59	3.50	3.40
20	.05	5.60	4.59	4.01	3.80	3.62	3.46	3.38	3.30	3.23	3.16	3.09	3.02
	.01	8.00	6.08	5.06	4.73	4.42	4.15	4.04	3.90	3.79	3.69	3.58	3.48
25	.05	5.89	4.78	4.15	3.93	3.74	3.55	3.47	3.39	3.31	3.24	3.16	3.09
	.01	8.37	6.30	5.20	4.86	4.53	4.25	4.1*	3.98	3.88	3.76	3.64	3.54
30	.05	6.15	4.95	4.27	4.04	3.82	3.63	3.54	3.46	3.38	3.30	3.22	3.15
	.01	8.68	6.49	5.33	4.95	4.61	4.33	4.2*	4.13	3.93	3.81	3.69	3.59
35	.05	6.36	5.09	4.37	4.13	3.90	3.70	3.61	3.52	3.43	3.34	3.27	3.19
	.01	8.95	6.67	5.44	5.04	4.71	4.39	4.3*	4.26	3.97	3.84	3.73	3.63
40	.05	6.56	5.21	4.45	4.20	3.97	3.76	3.66	3.57	3.48	3.39	3.31	3.23
	.01	9.19	6.83	5.52	5.12	4.78	4.46	4.3*	4.1*	4.01	3.89	3.77	3.66
45	.05	6.70	5.31	4.53	4.26	4.02	3.80	3.70	3.61	3.51	3.42	3.34	3.26
	.01	9.41	6.93	5.60	5.20	4.84	4.52	4.3*	4.2*	4.1*	3.93	3.80	3.69
50	.05	6.86	5.40	4.59	4.32	4.07	3.85	3.74	3.65	3.55	3.46	3.37	3.29
	.01	9.68	7.06	5.70	5.27	4.90	4.56	4.4*	4.2*	4.1*	3.97	3.83	3.72
100	.05	8.00	6.08	5.06	4.73	4.42	4.15	4.04	3.90	3.79	3.69	3.58	3.48
	.01	11.04	7.80	6.20	5.70	5.20	4.80	4.7*	4.4*	4.5*		4.00	3.89
250	.05	9.68	7.06	5.70	5.27	4.90	4.56	4.4*	4.2*	4.1*	3.97	3.83	3.72
	.01	13.26	8.83	6.9*	6.3*	5.8*	5.2*	5.0*	4.9*	4.8*			4.11

SOURCE: From "Multiple Comparisons Among Means," *Journal of the American Statistical Association, 56,* 52-64, by O. J. Dunn, copyright © 1961 by the American Statistical Association, as adapted by R. E. Kirk, *Experimental Design: Procedures for the Behavioral Sciences,* second edition, Brooks/Cole Publishing Company, 1982. Reprinted with permission from the American Statistical Association and Brooks/Cole Publishing Company, Pacific Grove, CA 93950.

*Obtained by graphical interpolation.

TABLE E

Critical Values for Dunnett: Percentage Points for the Comparison of $J - 1$ Treatment Means With a Control

One-Tailed Comparisons

Error df	α	Number of Treatment Means, Including Control (J)								
		2	3	4	5	6	7	8	9	10
5	.05	2.02	2.44	2.68	2.85	2.98	3.08	3.16	3.24	3.30
	.01	3.37	3.90	4.21	4.43	4.60	4.73	4.85	4.94	5.03
6	.05	1.94	2.34	2.56	2.71	2.83	2.92	3.00	3.07	3.12
	.01	3.14	3.61	3.88	4.07	4.21	4.33	4.43	4.51	4.59
7	.05	1.89	2.27	2.48	2.62	2.73	2.82	2.89	2.95	3.01
	.01	3.00	3.42	3.66	3.83	3.96	4.07	4.15	4.23	4.30
8	.05	1.86	2.22	2.42	2.55	2.66	2.74	2.81	2.87	2.92
	.01	2.90	3.29	3.51	3.67	3.79	3.88	3.96	4.03	4.09
9	.05	1.83	2.18	2.37	2.50	2.60	2.68	2.75	2.81	2.86
	.01	2.82	3.19	3.40	3.55	3.66	3.75	3.82	3.89	3.94
10	.05	1.81	2.15	2.34	2.47	2.56	2.64	2.70	2.76	2.81
	.01	2.76	3.11	3.31	3.45	3.56	3.64	3.71	3.78	3.83
11	.05	1.80	2.13	2.31	2.44	2.53	2.60	2.67	2.72	2.77
	.01	2.72	3.06	3.25	3.38	3.48	3.56	3.63	3.69	3.74
12	.05	1.78	2.11	2.29	2.41	2.50	2.58	2.64	2.69	2.74
	.01	2.68	3.01	3.19	3.32	3.42	3.50	3.56	3.62	3.67
13	.05	1.77	2.09	2.27	2.39	2.48	2.55	2.61	2.66	2.71
	.01	2.65	2.97	3.15	3.27	3.37	3.44	3.51	3.56	3.61
14	.05	1.76	2.08	2.25	2.37	2.46	2.53	2.59	2.64	2.69
	.01	2.62	2.94	3.11	3.23	3.32	3.40	3.46	3.51	3.56
15	.05	1.75	2.07	2.24	2.36	2.44	2.51	2.57	2.62	2.67
	.01	2.60	2.91	3.08	3.20	3.29	3.36	3.42	3.47	3.52
16	.05	1.75	2.06	2.23	2.34	2.43	2.50	2.56	2.61	2.65
	.01	2.58	2.88	3.05	3.17	3.26	3.33	3.39	3.44	3.48
17	.05	1.74	2.05	2.22	2.33	2.42	2.49	2.54	2.59	2.64
	.01	2.57	2.86	3.03	3.14	3.23	3.30	3.36	3.41	3.45
18	.05	1.73	2.05	2.21	2.32	2.41	2.48	2.53	2.58	2.62
	.01	2.55	2.84	3.01	3.12	3.21	3.27	3.33	3.38	3.42
19	.05	1.73	2.03	2.20	2.31	2.40	2.47	2.52	2.57	2.61
	.01	2.54	2.83	2.99	3.10	3.18	3.25	3.31	3.36	3.40
20	.05	1.72	2.03	2.19	2.30	2.39	2.46	2.51	2.56	2.60
	.01	2.53	2.81	2.97	3.08	3.17	3.23	3.29	3.34	3.38
24	.05	1.71	2.01	2.17	2.28	2.36	2.43	2.48	2.53	2.57
	.01	2.49	2.77	2.92	3.03	3.11	3.17	3.22	3.27	3.31
30	.05	1.70	1.99	2.15	2.25	2.33	2.40	2.45	2.50	2.54
	.01	2.46	2.72	2.87	2.97	3.05	3.11	3.16	3.21	3.24
40	.05	1.68	1.97	2.13	2.23	2.31	2.37	2.42	2.47	2.51
	.01	2.42	2.68	2.82	2.92	2.99	3.05	3.10	3.14	3.18
60	.05	1.67	1.95	2.10	2.21	2.28	2.35	2.39	2.44	2.48
	.01	2.39	2.64	2.78	2.87	2.94	3.00	3.04	3.08	3.12
120	.05	1.66	1.93	2.08	2.18	2.26	2.32	2.37	2.41	2.45
	.01	2.36	2.60	2.73	2.82	2.89	2.94	2.99	3.03	3.06
∞	.05	1.64	1.92	2.06	2.16	2.23	2.29	2.34	2.38	2.42
	.01	2.33	2.56	2.68	2.77	2.84	2.89	2.93	2.97	3.00

SOURCE: The part of this table presenting one-tailed comparisons is from "A Multiple Comparison Procedure for Comparing Several Treatments With a Control," ***Journal of the American Statistical Association, 50,*** **1096-1121, by C. W. Dunnett, copyright © 1955 by the American Statistical Association, as adapted by R. E. Kirk,** ***Experimental Design: Procedures for the Behavioral Sciences,*** **second**

TABLE E
Continued

Two-Tailed Comparisons

Error df	α	Number of Treatment Means, Including Control (J) 2	3	4	5	6	7	8	9	10
5	.05	2.57	3.03	3.29	3.48	3.62	3.73	3.82	3.90	3.97
	.01	4.03	4.63	4.98	5.22	5.41	5.56	5.69	5.80	5.89
6	.05	2.45	2.86	3.10	3.26	3.39	3.49	3.57	3.64	3.71
	.01	3.71	4.71	4.51	4.71	4.87	5.00	5.10	5.20	5.28
7	.05	2.36	2.75	2.97	3.12	3.24	3.33	3.41	3.47	3.53
	.01	3.50	3.95	4.21	4.39	4.53	4.64	4.74	4.82	4.89
8	.05	2.31	2.67	2.88	3.02	3.13	3.22	3.29	3.35	3.41
	.01	3.36	3.77	4.00	4.17	4.29	4.40	4.48	4.56	4.62
9	.05	2.26	2.61	2.81	2.95	3.05	3.14	3.20	3.26	3.32
	.01	3.25	3.63	3.85	4.01	4.12	4.22	4.30	4.37	4.43
10	.05	2.23	2.57	2.76	2.89	2.99	3.07	3.14	3.19	3.24
	.01	3.17	3.53	3.74	3.88	3.99	4.08	4.16	4.22	4.28
11	.05	2.20	2.53	2.72	2.84	2.94	3.02	3.08	3.14	3.19
	.01	3.11	3.45	3.65	3.79	3.89	3.98	4.05	4.11	4.16
12	.05	2.18	2.50	2.68	2.81	2.90	2.98	3.04	3.09	3.14
	.01	3.05	3.39	3.58	3.71	3.81	3.89	3.96	4.02	4.07
13	.05	2.16	2.48	2.65	2.78	2.87	2.94	3.00	3.06	3.10
	.01	3.01	3.33	3.52	3.65	3.74	3.82	3.89	3.94	3.99
14	.05	2.14	2.46	2.63	2.75	2.84	2.91	2.97	3.02	3.07
	.01	2.98	3.29	3.47	3.59	3.69	3.76	3.83	3.88	3.93
15	.05	2.13	2.44	2.61	2.73	2.82	2.89	2.95	3.00	3.04
	.01	2.95	3.25	3.43	3.55	3.64	3.71	3.78	3.83	3.88
16	.05	2.12	2.42	2.59	2.71	2.80	2.87	2.92	2.97	3.02
	.01	2.92	3.22	3.39	3.51	3.60	3.67	3.73	3.78	3.83
17	.05	2.11	2.41	2.58	2.69	2.78	2.85	2.90	2.95	3.00
	.01	2.90	3.19	3.36	3.47	3.56	3.63	3.69	3.74	3.79
18	.05	2.10	2.40	2.56	2.68	2.76	2.83	2.89	2.94	2.98
	.01	2.88	3.17	3.33	3.44	3.53	3.60	3.66	3.71	3.75
19	.05	2.09	2.39	2.55	2.66	2.75	2.81	2.87	2.92	2.96
	.01	2.86	3.15	3.31	3.42	3.50	3.57	3.63	3.68	3.72
20	.05	2.09	2.38	2.54	2.65	2.73	2.80	2.86	2.90	2.95
	.01	2.85	3.13	3.29	3.40	3.48	3.55	3.60	3.65	3.69
24	.05	2.06	2.35	2.51	2.61	2.70	2.76	2.81	2.86	2.90
	.01	2.80	3.07	3.22	3.32	3.40	3.47	3.52	3.57	3.61
30	.05	2.04	2.32	2.47	2.58	2.66	2.72	2.77	2.82	2.86
	.01	2.75	3.01	3.15	3.25	3.33	3.39	3.44	3.49	3.52
40	.05	2.02	2.29	2.44	2.54	2.62	2.68	2.73	2.77	2.81
	.01	2.70	2.95	3.09	3.19	3.26	3.32	3.37	3.41	3.44
60	.05	2.00	2.27	2.41	2.51	2.58	2.64	2.69	2.73	2.77
	.01	2.66	2.90	3.03	3.12	3.19	3.25	3.29	3.33	3.37
120	.05	1.98	2.24	2.38	2.47	2.55	2.60	2.65	2.69	2.73
	.01	2.62	2.85	2.97	3.06	3.12	3.18	3.22	3.26	3.29
∞	.05	1.96	2.21	2.35	2.44	2.51	2.57	2.61	2.65	2.69
	.01	2.58	2.79	2.92	3.00	3.06	3.11	3.15	3.19	3.22

edition, Brooks/Cole Publishing Company, 1982. Reprinted by permission of the American Statistical Association and Brooks/Cole Publishing Company, Pacific Grove, CA 93950. The part of the table presenting two-tailed comparisons is from C. W. Dunnett, "New Tables for Multiple Comparisons With a Control," *Biometrics, 20,* 482-491, copyright © 1964 by the Biometric Society, as adapted by R. E. Kirk, *Experimental Design: Procedures for the Behavioral Sciences,* second edition, Brooks/Cole Publishing Company, 1982. Reprinted with permission of the Biometric Society and Brooks/Cole Publishing Company, Pacific Grove, CA 93950.

NOTES

1. Space limitations prevent thorough coverage of ANOVA, and it is assumed that you know the terminology and notation (e.g., F, SS, MS, df). See Iversen and Norpoth (1987) for details.

2. This example is based on Staub (1970), and the data in Table 1.1 were simulated to give interesting results for this example.

3. That is, a weighted sum of the means, where the weights are symbolized as c_j's. Note that this weighted sum, or comparison, exists only for fixed means, and thus only for the fixed effects model ANOVA.

4. Many of the classifications given here are taken from Toothaker (1986).

5. The term *orthogonal* is being used here in spite of the popular use in multiple comparison literature of the term *independent*. As will be shown later in this chapter, what is of concern is if $\Sigma c_{1j}c_{2j} = 0$, which demonstrates orthogonality. If $\Sigma c_j = 0$, as is always the case for multiple comparisons, then orthogonality, $\Sigma c_{1j}c_{2j} = 0$, also makes the two comparisons linearly independent and uncorrelated (see Rodgers, Nicewander, & Toothaker, 1984).

6. Controlling error rate per comparison can also be referred to as a *comparisonwise* approach to error rate control. Proponents of this approach include Carmer and Walker (1982), O'Brien (1983), and Rothman (1990).

7. Just as there are different types of error rate for multiple comparisons, there are also different types of power: any pair power, all pairs power, and per pair power (see Toothaker, 1991). These different types of power are useful to multiple comparison researchers, but have less utility for users of multiple comparison procedures.

8. A fairly strong argument can be made that examination of powers of methods should take place only for those methods that control α in a similar manner. I agree with this argument, but still recognize the elementary principle that higher α gives higher power.

9. Some authors choose to use the word *experiment* in place of *family* in discussing error rate. Since some experiments will contain more than one family of comparisons, such as a two-way ANOVA, I prefer the term *family*.

10. Some statistics for MCPs cannot be interchanged. There exists a multiple F statistic approach that uses tests of equality of means in sets rather than a test of the difference between two means (see Toothaker, 1991).

11. The Studentized range, q, is a statistic defined as the difference (range) between two variables divided by an estimator of the standard deviation of one of the variables. Dividing by the estimator of the standard deviation is said to "Studentize" the range. Thus $(X_i - X_j)/s$ is a Studentized range (q) statistic where the X's are raw scores. As applied in MCPs, the difference is a range of sample means that is divided by the estimated standard deviation of a sample mean, $\sqrt{\text{MS}_W/n}$, an estimator of $\sqrt{\sigma^2/n}$, the standard error of the mean. If the variables are J independent, unit normal, random variables divided by the square root of an independent chi-square divided by its degrees of freedom, then the q statistic has the Studentized range distribution. The Studentized range distribution will be discussed further in Chapter 2.

12. The F statistic discussed here is not the result of an ANOVA on J means, but a simple transformation of the t statistic on two means.

13. Any equivalent word could be used instead of *contain,* such as *include* or *bracket.*

14. Orthogonality is an important concept in many other areas of statistics, such as its use in two-way and higher ANOVA when equal sample sizes are present. Also, orthogonality of comparisons has utility in consideration of the design matrix for use of the general linear model approach for ANOVA. But if you use multiple comparisons in the way discussed in this book, orthogonality of comparisons becomes a secondary issue against the backdrop of the more weighty matters of control of α and power. That is, you should let your comparisons be whatever the research dictates, orthogonal or not, and you should focus your attention on controlling α and choosing a powerful multiple comparison method.

15. If sample sizes are unequal, then the requirement for orthogonality of two comparisons is $\Sigma c_{1j}c_{2j}/n_j = 0$.

16. While the MCPs in this text are given in terms of two-tailed tests of nondirectional hypotheses, some of them can be used easily as one-tailed tests if direction is predicted in the alternative hypothesis. Those MCPs that offer this option are the *usual t,* Dunn, by using 2α, and Dunnett, by using a special table.

17. Modifications of Dunn's method that are sequential and thus not STPs will not be covered in this text. See Toothaker (1991), Holm (1979), and Shaffer (1986) for these sequential procedures that divide up α.

18. Dunn (1958) and Šidák (1967) developed another MCP by using the idea of setting $\alpha'' = 1 - (1 - \alpha)^{1/C}$. There is a slight power gain when using this MCP over use of the Dunn. Special tables are needed for the Dunn-Šidák (see Games, 1977; Kirk, 1982; Toothaker, 1991).

19. The test credited to Dunn divides up α evenly, although this is not necessary. Another approach would be to set the α' at values that add up to α, such as four comparisons at $\alpha' = .005$ and one at $\alpha' = .03$, giving a total of $\alpha = .05$. The approach that allows unequal division of α is often called the Bonferroni method, and does not have any standard tables.

20. Tukey's test is often referred to as the *honestly significant difference* (HSD) test or the *wholly significant difference* (WSD) test. Another name sometimes given to the Tukey test is Tukey (a) because he developed a second test called Tukey (b).

21. The Studentized range distribution controls α for the entire set of comparisons on J means because it gives critical values for the distribution of the maximum $(Y_j - Y_{j'})/(s/\sqrt{N})$. Since it controls for the maximum difference in the J means, it controls for all the pairwise comparisons.

22. Some authors refer to stepwise procedures as *layered* procedures.

23. Welsch (1977a, 1977b), Hochberg (1988), and Dunnett and Tamhane (1992) have presented methods that are step-up MCPs. For pairwise comparisons, step-up logic starts with statistics for the $p = 2$ comparisons and compares them to a critical value. If a comparison is significant, then all comparisons containing the significant comparison are declared significant by implication. Nonsignificant lower stretch comparisons simply lead to direct testing of the higher stretch comparisons not already declared significant by implication to see if they are significant when compared to appropriate critical values. Comparisons at stretch size $p > 2$ proceed in a similar fashion of comparing a statistic to a critical value and if the comparison is significant, declaring all comparisons containing the significant comparison as significant by implication.

Note that step-up logic declares significance by implication in contrast to declaration of nonsignificance by implication for step-down logic. These step-up methods will not be presented in this book.

24. Some authors refer to the way Newman-Keuls controls α as a *p*-mean significance level, since it controls α for a set of *p* equal means (e.g., Miller, 1981, p. 85).

25. An additional procedure that could be considered an extension of the Ryan MCP is due to Peritz (1970). It is computer-intensive and is not available on SAS or SPSS. See Toothaker (1991) for details.

26. Hayter (1986) has shown that for $J = 4$, the p(at least one Type I error) for the protected *t* test is .1222 for $\alpha = .05$. The probability increases as a function of *J*, and for $J = 10$ is .5715 for $\alpha = .05$.

27. For example, *C* could be chosen to be a large value and type of comparison could be nonpairwise comparisons. Then only Dunn and Scheffé would be appropriate to compare, because the other MCPs are used only for pairwise comparisons.

28. Of course, the ANOVA assumptions are on the error component of the linear model, but, since it is a fixed-effects model, the assumptions also apply to the observed score in the model. Thus it is accurate to say that the data have the same three assumptions of normality, equal variances, and independence.

29. The Behrens-Fisher problem for independent samples is one of testing for equality of two population means when the population variances are unknown and potentially unequal.

30. Technically, kurtosis is peakedness relative to the normal distribution, but a highly peaked distribution often has long tails. That is, it has outliers in both tails if it is symmetrical. Of course, a distribution can be both peaked and skewed.

31. For a summary of robust estimation in MCPs, see Hochberg and Tamhane (1987, pp. 271-273).

32. As was the case for the one-way ANOVA, I assume that you have had an introduction to the two-way ANOVA.

33. The data presented here were simulated to have exactly the same means and standard deviations as given in Frank (1984), and thus give the same results on the overall *F*'s.

34. Because both block and treatment would be regarded as fixed in this example, the MS_W is the correct denominator for the *F*'s and the subsequent MCPs.

35. At this point, the name for the statistical procedure, *two-way ANOVA,* will be used for any experimental design that uses this procedure. Thus this generic title will stand for a factorial arrangement of two treatments, commonly called a factorial design, or a randomized block design where both treatment and block factors are fixed. For MCPs in repeated measures designs, see Toothaker (1991) or Kirk (1982).

36. The real issue is what question is being asked by most researchers. Is it about means or interaction effects? Levin and Marascuilo (1972) suggest that the overall *F* test might be bypassed altogether. Since most researchers are ultimately interested in the cell means tests, this suggestion is quite appropriate: The overall two-way ANOVA is rarely a good picture of the ultimately desired analysis. Usually it is run merely out of habit, tradition, or convenience, or to obtain some of the statistics needed for the MCPs. The reason most researchers prefer tests on cell means is that the overall ANOVA and the test of interaction do not represent the researchers' questions.

37. Those wanting to do tests on interaction effects should see Rosnow and Rosenthal (1989) or Marascuilo and Levin (1970). Good coverage of the methods by which to partition SS_{AB} is also given in Kirk (1982, p. 371) under the title of "treatment-contrast interactions."

38. Similar parameters exist for the critical values for some other MCPs, such as the number-of-means minus one for Scheffé, which was $J - 1$ for the one-way ANOVA. These

parameters are always related to the number-of-means parameter for the Studentized range. However, note that it is difficult to conceive of the Ryan MCP for cell means because of the requirement of ordering the means. Finally, note that Dunn does not need a number-of-means parameter because it uses the number of comparisons actually computed, *C*.

39. Some authors recommend using $\alpha = .05 + .05 = .10$ as the total α for these tests, recognizing that they are MCPs done on *simple effects* and, as such, add together the sources of variability from one main effect and the interaction. Since the original *F* tests on these effects are done at the $\alpha = .05$ level, the logic is that the α's should also be added. Note that this decision is made regardless of the decision about the number-of-means parameter.

REFERENCES

BRAY, J. H., and MAXWELL, S. E. (1985) Multivariate Analysis of Variance. Sage University Paper series on Quantitative Applications in the Social Sciences, 07-054. Newbury Park, CA: Sage.

BROWN, S. R., and MELAMED, L. E. (1990) Experimental Design and Analysis. Sage University Paper series on Quantitative Applications in the Social Sciences, 07-074. Newbury Park, CA: Sage.

CARMER, S. G., and WALKER, W. M. (1982) "Baby Bear's dilemma: A statistical tale." Agronomy Journal 74: 122-124.

CICCHETTI, D. V. (1972) "Extension of multiple-range tests to interaction tables in the analysis of variance: A rapid approximate solution." Psychological Bulletin 77: 405-408.

CONOVER, W. J., and IMAN, R. L. (1981) "Rank transformations as a bridge between parametric and nonparametric statistics." American Statistician 35: 124-133.

DUNCAN, D. B. (1955) "Multiple range and multiple *F* tests." Biometrics 11: 1-42.

DUNN, O. J. (1958) "Estimation of the means of dependent variables." Annals of Mathematical Statistics 29: 1095-1111.

DUNN, O. J. (1961) "Multiple comparisons among means." Journal of the American Statistical Association 56: 52-64.

DUNNETT, C. W. (1955) "A multiple comparison procedure for comparing several treatments with a control." Journal of the American Statistical Association 50: 1096-1121.

DUNNETT, C. W. (1980) "Pairwise multiple comparisons in the unequal variance case." Journal of the American Statistical Association 75: 796-800.

DUNNETT, C. W. (1982) "Robust multiple comparisons." Communications in Statistics 11: 2611-2629.

DUNNETT, C. W., and TAMHANE, A. C. (1992) "A step-up multiple test procedure." Journal of the American Statistical Association 87: 162-170.

EINOT, I., and GABRIEL, K. R. (1975) "A study of the powers of several methods of multiple comparisons." Journal of the American Statistical Association 70: 574-583.

FISHER, R. A. (1935) The Design of Experiments. Edinburgh: Oliver & Boyd.

FRANK, B. M. (1984) "Effect of field independence-dependence and study technique on learning from a lecture." American Educational Research Journal 21: 669-678.

FRENCH, J. W., EKSTROM, R. B., and PRICE, L. A. (1963) Manual for Kit of Reference Tests for Cognitive Factors. Princeton, NJ: Educational Testing Service.

GAMES, P. A. (1973) "Type IV errors revisited." Psychological Bulletin 80: 304-307.

GAMES, P. A. (1977) "An improved *t* table for simultaneous control on *g* contrasts." Journal of the American Statistical Association 72: 531-534.

GAMES, P. A., and HOWELL, J. F. (1976) "Pairwise multiple comparison procedures with unequal *n*'s and/or variances." Journal of Educational Statistics 1: 113-125.

GIRDEN, E. R. (1992) ANOVA: Repeated Measures. Sage University Paper series on Quantitative Applications in the Social Sciences, 07-084. Newbury Park, CA: Sage.

HAYTER, A. J. (1986) "The maximum familywise error rate of Fisher's least significant difference test." Journal of the American Statistical Association 81: 1000-1004.

HOCHBERG, Y. (1988) "A sharper Bonferroni procedure for multiple tests of significance." Biometrika 75: 800-802.

HOCHBERG, Y., and TAMHANE, A. C. (1987) Multiple Comparison Procedures. New York: John Wiley.

HOLM, S. (1979) "A simple sequentially rejective multiple test procedure." Scandinavian Journal of Statistics 6: 65-70.

IVERSEN, G. R., and NORPOTH, H. (1987) Analysis of Variance (2nd ed.). Sage University Paper series on Quantitative Applications in the Social Sciences, 07-001. Newbury Park, CA: Sage.

KESELMAN, H. J., GAMES, P. A., and ROGAN, J. C. (1979) "An addendum to 'A comparison of modified-Tukey and Scheffé methods of multiple comparisons for pairwise contrasts.' " Journal of the American Statistical Association 74: 626-627.

KESELMAN, H. J., and ROGAN, J. C. (1978) "A comparison of modified-Tukey and Scheffé methods of multiple comparisons for pairwise contrasts." Journal of the American Statistical Association 73: 47-51.

KESELMAN, H. J., and TOOTHAKER, L. E. (1974) "Comparison of Tukey's T-method and Scheffé's S-method for various numbers of all possible differences of averages contrasts under violation of assumptions." Educational and Psychological Measurement 34: 511-519.

KESELMAN, H. J., TOOTHAKER, L. E., and SHOOTER, M. (1975) "An evaluation of two unequal n_k forms of the Tukey multiple comparison statistic." Journal of the American Statistical Association 70: 584-587.

KEULS, M. (1952) "The use of the 'Studentized range' in connection with an analysis of variance." Euphytica 1: 112-122.

KIRK, R. E. (1982) Experimental Design: Procedures for the Behavioral Sciences. Belmont, CA: Brooks/Cole.

KLOCKARS, A. J., and SAX, G. (1986) Multiple Comparisons. Sage University Paper series on Quantitative Applications in the Social Sciences, 07-061. Newbury Park, CA: Sage.

KRAMER, C. Y. (1956) "Extension of multiple range test to group means with unequal numbers of replications." Biometrics 12: 307-310.

KRAMER, C. Y. (1957) "Extension of multiple range tests to group correlated adjusted means." Biometrics 13: 13-18.

LEVIN, J. R., and MARASCUILO, L. A. (1972) "Type IV errors and interactions." Psychological Bulletin 78: 368-374.

LEVIN, J. R., and MARASCUILO, L. A. (1973) "Type IV errors and Games." Psychological Bulletin 80: 308-309.

MARASCUILO, L. A., and LEVIN, J. R. (1970) "Appropriate post hoc comparisons for interaction and nested hypotheses in analysis of variance designs: The elimination of Type IV errors." American Educational Research Journal 7: 397-421.

MARASCUILO, L. A., and LEVIN, J. R. (1976) "The simultaneous investigation of interaction and nested hypotheses in two-factor analysis of variance designs." American Educational Research Journal 13: 61-65.

MARTIN, S. A., TOOTHAKER, L. E., and NIXON, S. J. (1989, April) "A Monte Carlo comparison of multiple comparison procedures under optimal and nonoptimal conditions." Presented at the annual meeting of the Southwestern Psychological Association, Houston.

MILLER, R. G. (1981) Simultaneous Statistical Inference (2nd ed.). New York: Springer-Verlag.

NEWMAN, D. (1939) "The distribution of the range in samples from a normal population, expressed in terms of an independent estimate of standard deviation." Biometrika 31: 20-30.

O'BRIEN, P. C. (1983) "The appropriateness of analysis of variance and multiple comparison procedures." Biometrics 39: 787-788.

PERITZ, E. (1970) "A note on multiple comparisons." Unpublished manuscript, Hebrew University, Israel.

PETRINOVICH, L. F., and HARDYCK, C. D. (1969) "Error rates for multiple comparison methods." Psychological Bulletin 71: 43-54.

RAMSEY, P. H. (1978) "Power differences between pairwise multiple comparisons." Journal of the American Statistical Association 73: 479-485.

RAMSEY, P. H. (1981) "Power of univariate pairwise multiple comparison procedures." Psychological Bulletin 90: 352-366.

RINGLAND, J. T. (1983) "Robust multiple comparisons." Journal of the American Statistical Association 78: 145-151.

RODGERS, J. L., NICEWANDER, W. A., and TOOTHAKER, L. E. (1984) "Linearly independent, orthogonal, and uncorrelated variables." American Statistician 38: 133-134.

ROSNOW, R., and ROSENTHAL, R. (1989) "Definition and interpretation of interaction effects." Psychological Bulletin 105: 143-146.

ROTHMAN, K. J. (1990) "No adjustments are needed for multiple comparisons." Epidemiology 1: 43-46.

RYAN, T. A. (1960) "Significance tests for multiple comparison of proportions, variance, and other statistics." Psychological Bulletin 57: 318-328.

SAS Institute, Inc. (1990) SAS/STAT User's Guide (vol. 1). Cary, NC: Author.

SAWILOWSKY, S. S., BLAIR, R. C., and HIGGINS, J. J. (1989) "An investigation of the Type I error and power properties of the rank transform procedure in factorial ANOVA." Journal of Educational Statistics 14: 255-267.

SCHEFFÉ, H. (1953) "A method for judging all contrasts in analysis of variance." Biometrika 40: 87-104.

SCHEFFÉ, H. (1959) The Analysis of Variance. New York: John Wiley.

SHAFFER, J. P. (1979) "Comparison of means: An *F* test followed by a modified multiple range procedure." Journal of Educational Statistics 4: 14-23.

SHAFFER, J. P. (1986) "Modified sequentially rejective multiple test procedures." Journal of the American Statistical Association 81: 826-831.

ŠIDÁK, Z. (1967) "Rectangular confidence regions for the means of multivariate normal distributions." Journal of the American Statistical Association 62: 626-633.

SPSS, Inc. (1990) SPSS Reference Guide. Chicago: Author.

STAUB, E. (1970) "A child in distress: The effect of focusing of responsibility on children on their attempts to help. Developmental Psychology 2: 152-153.

TAMHANE, A. C. (1979) "A comparison of procedures for multiple comparisons of means with unequal variances." Journal of the American Statistical Association 74: 471-480.

TOOTHAKER, L. E. (1986) Introductory Statistics for the Behavioral Sciences. New York: McGraw-Hill.

TOOTHAKER, L. E. (1991) Multiple Comparisons for Researchers. Newbury Park, CA: Sage.

TUKEY, J. W. (1953) "The problem of multiple comparisons." Mimeo.

WELCH, B. L. (1949) "Further note on Mrs. Aspin's tables and on certain approximations to the tabled functions." Biometrika 36: 293-296.

WELSCH, R. E. (1977a) "Stepwise multiple comparison procedures." Journal of the American Statistical Association 72: 566-575.

WELSCH, R. E. (1977b) "Tables for stepwise multiple comparison procedures." Unpublished manuscript, Massachusetts Institute of Technology.

ABOUT THE AUTHOR

LARRY E. TOOTHAKER is Professor of Psychology, University of Oklahoma, Norman, where he has taught since 1968. His research interests include multiple comparison procedures, repeated measures designs, robustness, outlier-resistant tests, and nonparametric methods. He has published articles in the *Journal of the American Statistical Association, Journal of Educational Statistics, Psychological Bulletin,* and other journals. He is the author of *Introductory Statistics for the Behavioral Sciences* (1986) and *Multiple Comparisons for Researchers* (1991), and has won numerous awards as a teacher of statistics and experimental design. In 1988, he was chosen as the outstanding professor in Oklahoma as the winner of the Gold Medal of Excellence in Teaching. In 1992, he was selected as a David Ross Boyd Professor, a lifelong honor for faculty members who have demonstrated outstanding teaching, guidance, and leadership for students at the University of Oklahoma. He was trained to be a high school mathematics teacher during his undergraduate work at the University of Nebraska, and his graduate work at the University of Wisconsin was in educational psychology.